I,Legal

in the U.S.A.

— a memoir —

by
ALEJANDRA CAMPOS

Published in the United States of America by *Skye's The Limit Publishing & Public Relations*

Books published by Skye's The Limit Publishing & Public Relations may be available at special discounts for bulk purchases in the United States by corporations, institutions, and other organizations. For more information, please contact the Marketing Department at Skye's The Limit Publishing & Public Relations, P.O. Box 133, Galena, Ohio 43021, (fax) 740-548-4929; or via e-mail at talk2stl@gmail.com

Declaration of Independence courtesy of the United States National Archives: http://www.archives.gov/exhibits/charters/charters_downloads.html

Cover, design, and typography by Cheryl A. Johnson

Skye's The Limit Publishing & Public Relations
PO Box 133, Galena, Ohio 43021
(fax) 740-548-4929
skyesthelimitpublishing.blogspot.com

Paperback (Full Color Deluxe Edition):
   ISBN-13: 978-1-939044-20-4
   ISBN-10: 1939044200

Paperback (Standard Black & White Edition):
   ISBN-13: 978-1-939044-21-1
   ISBN-10: 1939044219

Kindle eBook:
   ISBN-13: 978-1-939044-22-8

Book url: http://ilegal-intheusa.blogspot.com

Library of Congress Control Number: 2013946370

DISCLAIMER

The events, locales, and conversations contained in this book have been described according to the authors' memories, recognition, and understanding. Recollections from any given event can differ from one person to another. In order to protect the privacy of people involved in the events here described, some identifying details such as names, places, physical properties, and occupations have been changed.

PUBLISHER'S NOTE

Every possible effort has been made to ensure that the information contained in this book is accurate at the time of going to press, and the publisher and author cannot accept responsibility for any errors and omissions, however caused. No responsibility for loss or damage occasioned by any person acting, or refraining from action, as a result of the material in this publication can be accepted by the editor, the publisher, or the author.

To God who never left me.

And to Huseyin

for believing in me and my writing

when everybody else thought me crazy for trying.

Acknowledgements

This book would not have been possible without…

- Cheryl J. and Keith J. from Skye's The Limit Publishing & Public Relations whose knowledgeable input and invaluable help made this book a reality. It has been a pleasure working with you!

- All those who contributed with their pictures: Alvaro S., Alexia S. and Eugenia A.

- My "private detective" friends in San Salvador who took the time to answers my crazy questions regarding the city's current state: the amazing Monica V., Lissette V., and Blanca M. I am so blessed for having met you guys! You are amazing!

- My patient beta readers whose comments truly shaped the story: Alex M., Steffanie S., Normand S., Tracey L., Dorene M., Michael W., and Brandon M. Thank you for your time, comments, and feedback!

- The Memory to Memoirs Writer's Group: Gordon B., Alma G., Ann L., Louis S., and Mickie M. I learned a lot from all of you guys, thank you for welcoming me into your group.

- Andrew M., Alvaro A., Marta M., Ivonne G., Adrian A., Cindy R., Claudia K., Ray C., and Rosa M. for their encouragement and support.

- My U.S. "mom": Karen B. Words are not enough to express my gratitude for all your encouragement, patience, feedback, and overall awesomeness. Thank you so SO much for all!!!

- Huseyin A.: you know it…do you? Without you I would have never even started this project. Thank you for being there for me. You are the closest member of my family and very dear to me! I hope you never doubt this.

Note: Last names have been omitted to protect the contributors' identities.

Contents

To America With Love   Chapter 1

Dear American People:

If I told you that I am a Hispanic immigrant, what would you think of me?

If your guess is that I am a brown-skinned person who speaks with an accent, you are right. If you visualize me working in a fast food restaurant, or watering plants for somebody else's garden, again, you're right. I have done all of the above. I have also lived in houses that were infested with fleas, and spent many many evenings rummaging through the Salvation Army's clothing stores, full of joy, knowing that somewhere among the piles there lies a treasure: a second hand Banana Republic trouser or a GAP t-shirt whose wear and tear are minimal enough to make them pass as new—new to me at least.

What you might never imagine though, is that I am also an industrial engineer who graduated with honors from one of the most exclusive universities in Latin America; that the Ministry of Education in my country ranked me among the nation's top 1% of high school students and that I managed to complete a Master of Science program at The Ohio State University, with a nearly perfect score and without incurring any debt.

Contrary to what many may think, I have never in my life relied on welfare. I don't drink, don't smoke, don't use or deal drugs, am not promiscuous and am perfectly fluent in two languages.

The one thing I should add is that I have not broken any laws to be here. I am one of those "aliens" lucky enough to have a paper guaranteeing my legal status and, consequently, my rights as human being. So, my story is not going to be a terrible shocker; it is not going to involve people dying or suffocating in a truck while being smuggled across the border. The following pages are intended to show the <u>other</u> side of the story, the journey that *legal* immigrants have to go through and some of the often-unexpected challenges we have to face.

I should warn you: many of my views are controversial and some people may not like them, but please don't misunderstand me. The United States of America is a WONDERFUL country, the best I've ever seen and I'm very thankful for having been allowed in it. My intention is not to blame or criticize; I merely hope that by the end of this book you realize that (1) "Hispanic immigrant" is not a synonym of "uneducated," "dishwasher" or "criminal;" (2) Latin America is more than one country (not all of us are Mexicans) and (3) you are so SO lucky if you were born here, look white, or have English as your native language. As for the color, it's not that being white is better, by no means, we are all equal; but looking white certainly saves you a lot of trouble and prejudice.

What follows is a recollection of my memories, the impressions I've had as a Hispanic immigrant in the U.S.A. I don't intend to speak for any ethnic group, just for myself. If you've never had the opportunity to hear a Latina woman's perspective on the topic of "the American dream," consider this your chance. Get comfortable in your seat and let's have an honest conversation.

Where should we begin?

Volcan Izalco, El Salvador.
©2004, ogwen (http://flic.kr/p/6hnSL), under Creative Commons license (http://creativecommons.org/licenses/by/2.0/deed.en).

Why Do Hispanic Immigrants Keep Coming?   Chapter 2

That is a great question!

Before I tell you all there is to know about how I came legally to the U.S. and what my first impressions of the country were, I will tell you how life was in my hometown so that you can better understand the reasons that keep Hispanics like me coming. Keep in mind that I can only speak for what I've lived; I'm going to be 100% frank with you but, when it comes to points of view on immigration, they are as numerous and unique as those who immigrate.

The first thing I should say is that I come from El Salvador, a little country in Central America about one fifth the size of Ohio. My country has the dubious honor of being one of the most violent and unsafe in the world[1]. There you can get killed for wearing a gold chain in public. Using a flashy iPhone while walking on the streets? I wouldn't recommend it.

El Salvador's tropical weather is as warm as its people. The landscape is filled with natural beauties such as volcanoes, beaches, lakes and mountains, all in close proximity to each other. When I think of the year-long summers that I enjoyed there and all the good times I had with my friends, for a moment I wonder why I left. But then, I remember…

Salvadorians migrate for many reasons, I'm going to share with you what I think are the 3 main ones.

Reason No. 1: To Stop Living In Fear

Fear is a constant part of your existence when you live in El Salvador. From the moment you leave your house in the morning and wonder if you'll make it back, to the moment you lock all the doors at night, fear is always with you. When you grow up in the city, you get used to this state; the dread is eventually internalized and you replace the "I can die at any moment" feeling with a more tolerable "I should be careful at all times to be safe" which, of course, is a fallacy, because no matter how careful you are, tragedy can find you at any moment.

---

1 OSAC (The Overseas Security Advisory Council), 2012. El Salvador 2012 Crime and Safety Report. Bureau of Diplomatic Security, U.S. Department of State's. Available from: https://www.osac.gov/Pages/ContentReportDetails.aspx?cid=12336. Accessed on: 03/29/2013

Allow me to explain. Let's imagine for a minute that you are Sammy Salvadorian. You're a very dedicated parent of two who is offered the chance to work overtime on a Sunday night. Ever since baby Jimmy's birth you have been a little short of money, and thus you accept. Once the work is done, happy and satisfied, you head out to catch the bus that will take you home. As you ride, your mind wanders. Will Jesse cook eggs for dinner again? What should you do with the extra money you just earned? What bill should be paid first?…Little do you know that, after 15 minutes riding the bus, out of the blue and in the middle of the street, your vehicle is going to be stopped by a gang and, just because they feel like it, the gang members are going to set the bus on fire (with you inside) and, should you try to escape, they'll shoot you before you make it. They could even aim right at your knees to enjoy seeing you crawling, screaming, agonizing as your skin comes off in the fire. That is how sadistic they are. Oh, by the way, this is not a "what if" scenario. This actually happened a couple of years ago in my country. There were children in that bus[2].

In defense of the gang members, I have to say that they weren't doing it just for fun. You see, this is all part of their job. Any productive citizen of El Salvador who works hard and saves enough money to start a business, should include in his or her business plan a monthly stipend to cover the "rent" or "security fee" that the gangs charge in exchange for protection. Protection means that, if you pay them, they will not attack you. In the particular case above described, it was believed that the owners of the bus line had refused to pay. Initially, the gangs just detained the vehicles, had the people come out and burned the buses as reprisal; but when this failed to produce the rent payment, the next logical step was to burn the people alive. Simple, right? Yes, an easy and ordinary practice for the gangs in my country who can and do roam the streets with impunity.

If you think safety can be found inside people's houses, think twice. I can tell you this first hand. My Mom is an architect. She was a Fulbright scholar who obtained her master's degree in the U.S. When she returned to El Salvador, one of her projects involved the construction of a residential development with approximately 10 houses. With the profits, she designed and built the home of her dreams. It was a spacious two story house with service area for the sleep-in maid[3], three bathrooms, a huge master bedroom, and two extra rooms for my sister and me. When her house was finished, she stood up in front of it and admired her work. "Now," she thought, "I have everything I need to be happy."

The fairy tale ended the day robbers broke into our house. Despite having a garage door as a first barrier (see picture on page 7), the thieves skillfully climbed the walls and broke the front door open. They stole everything! I must admit that, in my innocence, I was kind of happy. Among their loot was an expensive violin Mom had bought and forced me to learn to play: I finally had an excuse to stop going to rehearsals!

---

2 Alex Renderos, 2010. 16 Killed in El Salvador bus attacks. *Los Angeles Times.* Available from: http://articles.latimes.com/2010/jun/21/world/la-fg-salvador-bus-20100622. Accessed on: 3/29/2013
3 Having maids back then was not uncommon for middle or upper-middle class families, given that maid wages were ridiculously low.

Had I been my Mom, I would have been terrified. I can imagine what it must be like for a divorced mother of two to realize she and her girls were not safe there anymore. But let me tell you something, my Mom is not one to scare easily; she is a truly remarkable woman. Instead of running away in panic, she quickly replaced the front door (which was made out of wood) with the best metal gate she could find. Try to open that *now* you low-lifes!

As expected, the thieves were not able to break through the front door anymore—they opened a hole through the roof instead, and thus a slow dance began between the owner of the house and the intruders. Not long after Mom had the ceiling covered with iron bars, they broke through the back garden. When she had razor wire installed in the garden, they broke through the service area. The tenacity of both parties was unbelievable!

A House
In The U.S.A.

Windows without bars

See-through Garage Door

- Front yards are generally open.
- Garages are used to store cars.
- Bars on windows are not common

A House
In El Salvador

Warning sign reads:
"High Voltage"

Razor wire

- Most houses are either surrounded by a wall or located within gated communities guarded by armed private security 24/7.
- Garage doors are used to gain access to the whole property inside.
- Most windows are covered with fixed metal bars. Barbed wire and electrified razor-blade wire are also used to prevent break-ins.

Every time a new break-in occurred, the police were called to the crime scene. They would efficiently cover every single nook in the house with their black dust, take finger prints, and scare the cat, but failed to produce any culprits. I was very little then and don't remember much more, but I do remember that the last time the men broke in was different…This time, when my family returned from a weekend trip, we sensed something was off. As we walked into the house, my Mom discovered, to her horror, that the scum bags had been waiting for us! They must have stayed there for a while because, in their boredom, they had used my Mom's lipsticks to draw obscene images of women on the wall and even left my mother the following message: *"Maria, where were you? We were waiting for you."*

Enough was enough. After that, we moved to a small apartment in a different part of the city. With neighbors living on top, below and next to us, we found safety in numbers. It makes me really sad to think how my Mom must have felt, her dreams shattered, so afraid. But she never showed us any fear or hesitation; she was always like a rock. She's always been my rock.

Why are the police unable to stop the violence? It could be the corruption or the lack of resources. I really don't know. There have been some attempts at controlling the situation but they all failed miserably. I remember the *Mano Dura* or "Heavy Hand" initiative the El Salvadorian government promoted some years ago. It gave our police increased power to detain and incarcerate suspected gang members based largely on their appearance, but the plan backfired when the gangs became more careful in their operations and harder to spot[4]. The government then responded with a "Super Heavy Hand" program which didn't fare any better. I found this all really hilarious, what was coming next? The "Extra-Super Heavy Hand"? As my great grandmother used to say: we should laugh instead of crying.

I hope by now you have a better idea of the first reason people may have to leave their countries. Remember: they do it in an attempt to stop living in fear.

Pharmacies, grocery stores, and most commercial establishments in El Salvador hire private security. Entrances to shopping centers, like the one in the picture, are also heavily guarded. If you are driving a car, a ticket is issued to you upon entering. If you fail to return the ticket on your way out, the authorities won't let you exit unless you show an ID and pay a fee. All this in hopes of preventing cars from being stolen from parking lots.

4   Clare Ribando Seelke, 2013. Gangs in Central America. Congresional Research Service. Available from: http://www.fas.org/sgp/crs/row/RL34112.pdf. Accessed on: 3/29/2013

Reason No. 2: For A Better Income And Quality Of Life

I recently stumbled across a chart with the minimum salaries established by the Ministry of Employment and Social Security in my home country[5]. Take a look at some of the numbers:

Minimum Salaries as of May 2011

Area of Work		Pay per day (U.S. $)	Pay per hour (U.S. $)
Harvesting	Coffee	3.82	0.478
	Sugar cane	3.24	0.405
	Cotton	2.92	0.365
Commerce and Services		7.47	0.934
Industry		7.31	0.914

Wow…What do you think? I wonder how many of us would be willing to break our backs working under the sun, collecting cotton by hand in an open field to get the astronomic sum of thirty six cents per hour. Can you imagine how the quality of your life would be if you were to earn less than three dollars per day?

If you earn $2.92 per *day* doing demanding work like this and you're told that you can earn $10 per *hour* cleaning someone else's house, what would you choose? Ten hours of sun burn, heat, bug bites, dirt, for $3.65; or 10 hours vacuuming climate-controlled houses for $100? This is the choice some of us have to make.

Please don't be under the impression that the cost of living in El Salvador is cheap enough to justify these meager salaries. Although the money paid to rent a house in El Salvador is considerably less than in the U.S., and the cost of human labor is also less, (think of a plumber, mechanic, etc.) everything else is almost equally priced, except gasoline which is more expensive. I have to acknowledge that a good percentage of the Salvadorian population have salaries above the minimum but, simply put, household incomes can easily be 20 times smaller than in the U.S. while the cost of living is not 20 times lesser — far from that![6]

We also have unemployment. The surest way to get a job in my country is by knowing someone, being somebody's son, brother, or best friend. Having the right connections you can go from sportscaster to president in El Salvador. It has happened![7] The problem is that most people don't know anyone important enough.

---

5   Ministry of Employment and Social Security, Republic of El Salvador, 2011. Minimum Salaries as of May 16th 2011. Official Journal No. 85, Volume 391, May 2011.

6   On May 2013 my friends reported the price of regular gasoline in El Salvador was $4.11 per gallon, a pound of cheap rice $0.66 and a MacDonald's "Big Mac" hamburger $3.35. The same day in the U.S.A. those items were priced at $3.69, $0.94 and $3.69 respectively (U.S. dollars).

7   Antonio Saca, 2013. Encyclopædia Britannica, Inc. Available from: http://www.britannica.com/EBchecked/topic/1013768/Antonio-Saca. Accessed on: 04/20/2013.

For many Salvadorians, living like this is not acceptable. Given the lawlessness that rules the country and the limited opportunities available for citizens to move forward, (open a business and deal with the gangs, study only to face unemployment, get employed and obtain a miserable salary) many choose to come to the U.S. To this day, a significant percentage of the country's Gross Domestic Product (GDP) comes from wire transfers from the United States. According to the CIA, remittances from our "far away brothers" represented 17% of the country's GDP in 2011 and were received by almost a third of all households.[8]

Reason No. 3: For A Healthier Environment

Safety and financial stability are obviously needed in order to have a good life. But, sometimes, the most important things for us happen to be those which we take for granted. Think about it, we may not even notice the air we're breathing, but take it away for a minute and we'll immediately remember its worth. That is often the case with a country's natural resources; and I am worried about El Salvador's. Let's take a brief look at its environmental situation.

Water and "El Espino"

El Salvador used to have a forest area called "El Espino" (The Hawthorn). It was a huge reserve that sheltered native flora and fauna, purified the air and, most importantly, served as a replenishment point for underground water supplies which are vital in a country with heavily contaminated rivers like ours.[9] During winter, rain would fall on the forest and infiltrate the ground, creating water reserves for the dry season.

Unfortunately, as the capital expanded, El Espino ended being right in the middle of it. The land became very valuable and, sooner rather than later, the private sector decided to get its hands on it. In an extremely questionable fashion which shocked environmental entities and was deemed unconstitutional by groups fighting it in the Supreme Court, large expansions of the forest were destroyed and replaced with luxury developments.[10] The area became the trendiest in town and is now filled with exclusive stores, restaurants and skyscraping condos. Nobody seems to remember there was ever a forest there and the destruction continues...

Not surprisingly, drinkable water is becoming an increasingly scarce commodity for San Salvador's population. Inadequate water supplies often force the city to stop pumping the liquid for days at a time. I suggest you try to live for a month limiting the use of your faucets and the flushing of your toilets to three times per week; that will give you a good idea of what this feels like. Then, if you succeed with the experiment, try imagining living like this for the rest of your life. Hint: you may find it a little uncomfortable.

8   Central Intelligence Agency (CIA), 2012. The World Factbook. Available from: https://www.cia.gov/library/publications/the-world-factbook/geos/es.html. Accessed on: 7/12/2012.

9   US Army Corps of Engineers, 1998. Water Resources Assessment of El Salvador. Mobile Disctrict & Topographic Engineering Center

10   Menjivar MD, Angel AA, Cubias ME., 1998. Analisis de la Legislacion Vigente en Relacion a la Deforestacion y su Incidencia Ambiental, en la Finca El Espino [University of El Salvador Thesis]. Corte Suprema de Justicia, Biblioteca Judicial "Dr. Ricardo Gallardo."

Let's Learn Some Lingo

For all our *hermanos lejanos* living in the U.S., especially the new generations who've never been in our Salvadorian country, let me show you some local words you should know about:

Hermano lejano = "Far away brother" for the millions of Salvadorians living out of the country. Did you know that about one fourth of Salvadorians live abroad and close to 80% of those who leave go to the United States?[1]

Bicho = "Bug" for young children. May have something to do with kids "bugging" parents.

Aguacateros = "Avocators," "Mutt" for the countless dogs that roam the streets freely. They are called avocators because they are hypothesized to survive by eating, among other unnamable things, the avocados that fall from the trees; much like squirrels eating nuts I guess.

A pack of 100% pure *Aguacatero* dogs takes a break after a day of begging for food inside The University of El Salvador. Students walk alongside the pack without paying attention to the utterly harmless animals.

1   Mary Beth Sheridan, 2004. Salvadoran Leader Embraces Diaspora, *The Washington Post*. Available from: http://www.washingtonpost.com/ac2/wp-dyn/A18428-2004Oct8?language=printer. Accessed on: 07/12/2012.

The great irony is that water is by no means absent in El Salvador. There is nearly 6 feet of rainfall each year![11,12] Where is all the water going???

Well, given that much of the land is now covered with cement, water cannot infiltrate the ground properly anymore and heads to the gutters instead. The copious amount of rain in the tropical country combined with unrestrained littering of the streets (which clogs the drains), conspire to turn the roads into improvised swimming pools. You should see the floods! If you're ever trapped in one of them, be careful with your driving. The muddy waters will not let you see anything underneath and you'll risk falling into one of our many pavement holes, or worst, into an open manhole! Desperate citizens often steal the covers to sell them as scrap metal and the manholes remain open for indefinite periods of time. The locals memorize the location of the holes and can easily avoid them, but if you are just visiting, beware.

Tanker trucks are sometimes hired by citizens to deliver water to their homes.

11 Hamilton J., 2005. Water Plentiful, But Contaminated in El Salvador. NPR. Available from: http://www.npr.org/templates/story/story.php?storyId=4983325 Accessed on: 3/30/2013
12 Universidad Centroamericana "Jose Simeon Cañas." 2011. Republica de El Salvador. Available from: http://www.uca.edu.sv/moea/el-salvador.php Accessed on: 3/30/2013

A Manhole In The U.S.A.

Metallic lids prevent the misfortune of innocent souls who drive or walk on top of manholes.

A Manhole In El Salvador

Lids are regularly stolen and sold as scrap metal.

Garbage and Bugs

Another topic that deserves to be mentioned is that of urban waste. It is embarrassing to admit it, but in my hometown there is little concern when it comes to littering public places. It may start with a guy throwing a candy wrap, another following with a plastic bag and, before you notice, huge dump sites start developing right next to your house. It is as if the first piece of trash felt lonely and started calling out for company.

The problem with garbage goes beyond street floods and aesthetics. Besides the unsightly view and rancid smell, improvised dumpsters are ideal breeding grounds for mosquitoes and other critters. When rain water accumulates in them, they turn into perfect nurseries for larvae. Once these hatch, there are clouds of them! Ugh…I almost get itchy at the thought. The worst is that if a mosquito bites you, it may give you dengue fever which can be fatal. And, since almost nobody has private medical insurance, people end up going to social security's hospitals which are perfect temples of doom (urban legends say that some patients are admitted for one thing and end up leaving with a different disease).

As superficial as this may sound, one of the things I am especially thankful for in the U.S. is the lack of mosquitoes and roaches. Oh yes!

I am aware this may differ according to the area in the country and many people will tell me they do have mosquito and roach issues but, so far, in all the places I have lived, I have never had to worry about hearing *that* buzz while I am sleeping at night. The dang mosquitoes somehow infiltrate the bedrooms and aim right at your ears, as if they were in love with the appendages and wanted to serenade them nightly as part of a courtship ritual; then, as soon as you turn the lights on to kill them, they disappear. If only they would just bite you on a foot and be done with it!…Ugh…and the roaches… those bugs are never ending, especially the flying kind. As a kid in my Mom's apartment, I had to run all over the place at least twice to escape from them; for some reason they always wanted to land on my head! I also remember that one morning I woke up to an itch on my back and, when I reached out to scratch it, the itch moved! It was a roach that had gotten in my pajamas!!!

Yes, I've had my share of close encounters with roaches, but I consider myself one of the lucky ones. When I was in high school there was a field trip to a landfill. The class was taken there to get acquainted with the "realities" of our country. I was not able to go, but my classmates came back telling me stories of all the "pepenadores" or waste scavengers who constantly roam the fields in search of items that can be sold as scrap. Some of them even live on the site and celebrate when, on certain days, waste trucks from restaurants arrive with half eaten pieces of chicken, left over French fries or discarded bread—true delicacies!

According to my classmates, the penetrating smell in the area was intolerable; it could be noticed miles away and impregnated people's clothes, hair, and skin to the point where a shower was needed to get rid of the stench. My friends said that those living on the site did not complain too much about it. I guess that, as with many things in life, you get used to it after a while.

Garbage Found In Residential Areas In The U.S.A.

- Waste often includes furniture and electronics (like the 50" television in the photo) in working condition — to my joy when I was a very poor student.
- Special containers are available for recyclable materials.

Garbage Found In Residential Areas In El Salvador

- Improvised dump sites "spawn" on their own.
- People search the garbage to find saleable items such as glass or aluminum.
- Police patrol the neighborhood.
- Commercial buses park in residential areas.
- Graffiti on the walls.

A Garbage Truck
In The U.S.A.

- Trucks are specially built for garbage collection (my eyes could not believe how clean this truck was when I took the picture).
- Garbage containers are specifically designed to be picked up by the truck's lift.
- People needed to collect the garbage this way: **ONE**, the driver.

A Garbage Truck
In El Salvador

- Garbage is often collected using regular trucks.
- Waste is placed in any type of containers such as plastic bags, sacks and boxes.
- People needed to collect the garbage, in this case: **SEVEN** — One driver, three workers who *run* alongside the truck picking up the trash, and three riding on top to receive and accommodate the bundles.

But All Problems Are Solved Once Immigrants Get Into The U.S., Right?

Well…Yes and no.

When our far away brothers visit El Salvador after a long absence, they normally do it loaded with gifts, dressed in their best clothes, and having a seemingly never ending supply of cash for entertainment.

Wonderful stories are told about the U.S.A., and those of us who hear them end up believing that North America is a wonderland where good things happen almost magically. The streets are practically covered with gold!

What our *hermanos lejanos* forget to emphasize, is where the money for their vacation is coming from, and how often they get to spend it with such unrestrained abandon. Those two weeks living large in El Salvador often come at the cost of years doing the hardest of labors.

The truth is that life after coming to the U.S. is not always rainbows and butterflies. It is not the paradise many hope to find—at least not right away—and it comes with its own load of issues. For starters, there is a clear distinction among races.

The Issue Of Race

You could say that it all began right around 1492 when arguably the first illegal immigrants, Cristobal Colon (AKA Christopher Columbus) and his European sailor friends, stumbled upon the "new world" and started what would later become a long process of colonization, looting and exploitation of the native people.

When Cristobal found America, it wasn't really lost—at least not to the people already living there. Cultures such as Mayans, Aztecs, and Incas (to name a few) who are often thought of as wild "tribes," were actually fairly advanced civilizations. They had knowledge of astronomy, engineering, mathematics, agriculture, their own religion, sports and culture. There was more to them than just a supposed prophecy of the end of the world in 2012.

Despite that, did you know that in some instances Europeans viewed natives as animals? Yes, large monkey-like creatures with no intelligence and maybe not even a soul[13]. That meant that killing them was no different from shooting deer during hunting season. On the other hand, when early groups of conquerors started coming from Spain, they were mistaken as deities by the natives! Since they were white, bearded (natives had no beard),[14] and had all sorts of ships and vestments the natives had never seen, they were believed to be emissaries from the gods, maybe even the gods themselves…what a mistake!

I don't intend to share a treatise on colonial history here, but my point is that whether we like it or not, whether this is politically correct or I'll forever burn for saying it, some of these perceptions of race inequality have permeated over time: there is a perceived superiority of the white race over the others in America. Here you go, I have said it. Now feel free to judge me and banish me to the dungeons of public shame.

---

13 Lewis Hanke, 1937. Pope Paul III and the American Indians. *Harvard Theological Review, 30*, pp 65-102
14 The Bearded White God of Ancient America: The legend of Quetzalcoatl [book].

Again, it is not that the white race is better or worse; I think we have enough geniuses, models and Nobel Prize winners from all ethnicities to prove that point, but the white race has the advantage of having been the *dominant* group, historically, in this continent. It was whites who colonized the Indians and brought African slaves; it was white railroad businessmen later taking advantage of Chinese. And I am not condemning or criticizing anyone, I am just stating some facts to help myself understand where these perceptions of superiority and inferiority are coming from.

If you go to El Salvador, you will soon notice that there are no Africans Americans, Indians, almost no Asians, and most of the people are mestiza[15]. About 9% of the population is white[16] but everybody else looks just about the same: brown skin, black hair, dark eyes. Now, I couldn't possibly deny the benefits of a multicultural society (in my opinion one of the main reasons for the U.S.A.'s success), but when you are a Hispanic living in El Salvador you don't particularly stand out, nobody judges you for your looks—unless of course you're a walking mess, but that is a different story. The point is that there are no pre-assigned racial labels of who you are expected to be.

That is not the case in the U.S. and, unfortunately, Hispanics don't fare all too well in the perceived status hierarchy, especially if illegal. Which brings us to…

The Issue Of Fear And Quality Of Life

We all have seen them, standing in the vicinity of home improvement stores waiting for the *patron*[17] of the day who will hire them as labor, flipping burgers in the kitchen of a fast-food restaurant, or cleaning that which nobody else wants to clean. Illegal immigrants, Hispanic immigrants, "Mexicans"…Have you seen them? I have.

As a matter of fact, I used to be one of them. Of course, I am not Mexican, and I'm definitely not illegal, but in my experience I have found that nationality and legal status in this country does not make much of a difference when you are newly arrived, speak with a strong Spanish accent, and lack the friends and connections needed to help you along the way.

Those who've ever traveled to a country without speaking the local language, ignoring the region's customs, and without a guide will probably understand me better. In those circumstances you can't help but feel foreign, lost, a little out of place. Now imagine if on top of that you know very well that you have broken the law to be there and the police are out to hunt you. This is what happens to illegals. They don't stop living in fear after coming to the U.S.—the sources of fear merely change and become more bearable. Instead of fearing being killed while walking on the street, they now fear being stopped by the police on the highway, or having a raid on their place of work. They fear deportation, they fear being caught and separated from their families. Some are even afraid to leave their houses and rarely do so if it isn't to buy groceries or go to work. What kind of life is that?

---

15 Racially mixed. As in Spanish American with American Indian.
16 Central Intelligence Agency, 2012. The World Factbook. Available from: https://www.cia.gov/library/publications/the-world-factbook/geos/es.html. Accessed on: 08/05/ 2012.
17 Boss, master.

As a legal immigrant I know deportation is not an issue I have to worry about every day, but I am concerned about all the prejudice. It seems to me that in this country Hispanics are tacitly distrusted and regarded as second-class inhabitants of the land. It is not something I can easily pin-point, nobody has openly discriminated against me based on my ethnicity (they know I could sue them for doing that), this is something that I feel from people's attitudes, reactions, and body language. You'd be surprised to know how many times I've been treated with undeserved hostility and wrongly judged by individuals who've only known me for a couple minutes. My English might not be perfect, but that doesn't mean I am mentally challenged as many assume. My skin may be dark, but that doesn't mean I'm dangerous. Also, it took a lot of effort and dedication to learn English; I don't understand why I'm more likely to be thought of as a criminal for having an accent than as a highly educated person for speaking two languages. Did I do something to deserve that?

At the end of the day though, this is a price we immigrants are willing to pay in exchange for the many advantages of being in this wonderful country. We know that, as long as we're here and if we work hard enough for it, we can hope to have that better future which is so often denied to us in our native lands.

The other day I read an article in the *Oprah* magazine that summarizes this point beautifully.[18] It says:

> For immigrants, heaven is minimum wage. Heaven is clean water. Heaven is an end to the constant threat of violence [...]. The heaven bar is pretty darn low, which is why so many immigrants embrace the thankless jobs most native-born Americans refuse to consider. If you can find paradise working in a meatpacking plant or emptying bedpans, imagine what your hell must have looked like.
>
> Now imagine raising your children there.

So, next time you hear that Hispanics keep coming to have a better life, I hope you remember that this "better" life is not necessarily an easy one; it's just that some of our countries are in such bad shape that, in many cases, pretty much *anything* is better.

---

18 Allison Glock, 2012. Hiding in Plain Sight: Inside the Life of an Undocumented Immigrant. *O, The Oprah Magazine*.

The Journey:
Tales Of Three Routes Of Death   Chapter 3

First Route Of Death

One of the earliest memories I have after coming to the U.S. is the clear image of me walking to the bus stop in the middle of the snow. It must have been really cold that day because my ears were getting numb.

Little did I know that this was just the beginning and that I would spend the next seven years freezing to the bone every winter. I always assumed that, being from a tropical country, my body was simply not made for those climates. Then, as an experiment to test my hypothesis once I had the money, I bought a $300 down coat and *¡santo remedio!* (holy remedy) the cold was gone.

The reason I remember this particular moment so clearly is that on that day I witnessed something I had never seen before and couldn't even imagine was possible. There it was: a public transportation bus that actually **stopped** at designated spots with perfect timing according to a schedule and, not only it waited for people to get in, but it LOWERED ITSELF down to floor level to allow senior citizens to board!!! I was in shock.

It was a "kneeling bus." The "beep, beep, beep" of the unit as it came closer to the ground took me by surprise. I looked around to see the reaction of everybody else at the bus stop but no one seemed astounded. So I pretended like it was normal for me too—it wasn't.

If you don't understand the reason of my amazement, let me tell you a little bit about buses in my Salvadorian country. Suffice it to say that one of the bus lines is fondly called "the route of death" by the people, due to the countless accidents that occur in it and the recklessness of the drivers.

A Public Transportation Bus In The U.S.A.

- Clean, climate-controlled interiors.
- Doors remain closed when the bus is in motion to ensure passenger safety.
- "Kneeling" buses can be lowered to ground level to facilitate boarding.
- Drivers wait for passengers to board before pulling away.
- Buses don't play scandalous background music.

A Public Transportation Bus
In El Salvador

- **Climate control mechanism**: opening the windows when it is too hot.
- Metallic bars installed around the door's exterior come in handy when buses are too full and passengers ride standing on the door's steps.
- Drivers constantly race against each other and thus can't wait for passengers to get in.
- Reggaeton music (Hispanic rap) blasts all day long in the background with explicit lyrics such as "Ride the *macho* baby" or "Tonight I'm gonna give her *rakata*."[19, 20]

---

19 "Macho" is slang for "male mule" but can also be used to designate a very masculine man. "Rakata" has no official meaning, it's just a sound.
20 For general culture, I refer you to YouTube, the song *El Gato Volador* (the flying cat) by "El Chombo," to have an idea of how Reggaeton sounds.

After years of practice, Salvadorians are well trained in the art of "grabbing-whatever-you-can" as soon as they place their first foot on a bus. Why? Because, drivers don't wait for people to get on. Oh no! Before passengers know it, the vehicle will start moving, and whoever is not quick enough to board will end up hanging outside the door. Sometimes, while grasping for a stable hold of some sort, guys end up "mistakenly" grabbing things that would be better left untouched. "*Mister! Be more careful please!*" say the girls when their butts are grabbed by surprise. Add to that a healthy dose of sexual deviants following you around in the crowd (closely, very closely) and you can imagine what an experience it is to ride our buses!

We look like sardines, and since ours is a very warm country all year long, those are some very sweaty sardines.

Second Route Of Death

Since this a book mainly about immigration, I cannot neglect to mention another route of death—one that is nothing to laugh about. That is, unfortunately, the route followed by illegal immigrants in pursuit of the American dream.

I have heard many times comments like *"These people should follow regular procedures to request the citizenship; why do they want to come illegally?"*…Jeez…please don't get angry at me for saying this but every time I hear these comments I get the creeps. I mean, how can anyone think that if there were any other viable option, illegals would choose to risk their life in such dangerous pursuit? I don't understand it; it must be that people in the U.S. don't really know all that is implied in coming here illegally.

If you are coming to the U.S. legally, you take a flight, enjoy your complimentary drink, and go from there. If you are entering illegally, the story is totally different. There are unscrupulous smugglers you must entrust your life to; in many cases women, girls, *and* boys have been molested by them. The trip is not just a few days; you're looking possibly at several months traveling by land in the most uncomfortable arrangements and in constant fear of being detained, because if you are, you will not only not reach your destination, you will also not get a refund. All the money you paid for the trip, which took years to save, is gone in a blink.

The worst is that you may also lose your life during the journey, seriously. Besides the risk of dying from exhaustion or dehydration in the desert, there are gangs and drug cartel organizations that have recently developed a penchant for kidnapping migrant groups and extorting them for money. One of my high school classmates, a journalist, recently made a documentary about this situation.[21] What she found left me speechless. She followed Hispanic immigrants coming from several regions in Central America. Apparently, when the travelers reach the Mexico/U.S.A. border, they are hunted like animals and held against their will by these criminal groups. When poor immigrants can't meet the kidnappers' demands, they are not only abused and tortured by their captors but *cut into pieces* that are disposed of in the most unnamable ways.[22] I would like to give you more details about this, but I consider the descriptions would be too gory and not suitable for young readers.

---

21 Marcela Zamora, 2010. "Maria in Nobody's Land." Human Rights Documentary, 2010. 86 min, MiniDV, Color.
22 Sanjuana Martinez, 2011. "Migrantes, el gran botin." DEMOS. Available from: http://www.jornada.unam.mx/2011/08/21/politica/002n1pol. Accessed on: 2013/04/01

Many books and documentaries have been made on this subject and my intention is not to retell that story here. I'll just say that the whole process is inhumane and serves as a rite of passage (no pun intended) for all the abuse that awaits illegal immigrants upon crossing the border.

So: No. It's not that we Latin people enjoy breaking the law; nor do we have an unusual desire to constantly live in fear of being pinpointed, taken to jail, and deported back to where we came from. No. The truth is that getting a legal status in the U.S. is just not that simple. It is not simple at all, and nearly impossible for the great majority.

In my case, my family was extremely lucky. Many years before I was born, one of my Mother's brothers had migrated to the States. He had been allowed to enter legally thanks to having medical skills in a time when the country had a shortage of doctors. Uncle Amaro was very intelligent, and eventually worked his way up becoming a well-established surgeon with resources to sponsor my Mother, my sister and me.

As far as I know it is not easy to be a sponsor, it is not easy to petition the government to grant your family a permanent legal status. For starters, you need to be in the country legally and prove that you have an adequate income to ensure that those you bring into the country will not rely on the U.S. government for financial support until they become citizens themselves (this takes at least 5 years)[23,24]. Not everybody is willing to commit this much, for this long, or has the resources to support a whole second family on top of their own.

There is also a limit on the number of relatives allowed to immigrate each year, so the waiting period before a visa becomes available is considerable[25]. Since my mother was an architect with a U.S. degree and none of us had diseases or criminal records, our application was accepted. It only took about 10 years for it to be approved. Luckily I was a toddler when the process began, so by the time I was a teenager, I was already a fortunate "green card" holder and thus was legally allowed to reside permanently in the U.S.A.

---

23 http://www.uscis.gov/portal/site/uscis - FORMS -- I-864, Affidavit of Support Under Section 213A of the Act
24 http://www.uscis.gov/portal/site/uscis -- FORMS -- USCIS - Path to U.S. Citizenship - USCIS Home Page
25 http://www.uscis.gov/portal/site/uscis -- FORMS -- Green Card for a Family Member of a U.S. Citizen

A Third Route Of Death: Mine

When I received my green card, I knew it was a privilege but I didn't know to what extent. I was a girl who had grown up in El Salvador under the impression that having roaches in one's home and metal bars on one's windows was not out of the ordinary. As a matter of fact, I never thought I'd end up leaving San Salvador. But, as they say: "Man proposes, God disposes." Here is my story…

According to Mom, when she divorced, my father said that it would be up to her to raise the children, and that he'd be responsible for two things: braces and college—it seems that teeth and education were very important to him. A man of his word, my father was absent most of my life. He cleverly developed a "remote" way to parent me. His system consisted in mailing one or two self-improvement books per year and otherwise pretending I didn't exist. At the end of each year, as if attempting to show "he cared," he'd pay for my sister and me to visit him in Panama (his place of residence). He'd take us to Disney World or to his house at the beach, but he always gave me this uncomfortable feeling of not wanting to be near me. He wouldn't talk to me, rarely answered my letters, and even if I was in Panama, he'd send me off to a different city as if avoiding the sight of me. Last time I visited him, he didn't even want to spend Christmas together! He had remarried and wanted to spend the holidays with his new family instead.

…My father was the first person who broke my heart.

Still, he kept his promise. Thanks to him my jaw was adjusted and my teeth straightened, and I am now the proud owner of a nice smile. Also, when I finished high school at the age of 16, he sent me to the prestigious "Monterrey Institute of Technology & Higher Education," a very expensive university in Mexico that Mom would have never been able to afford.

When I moved to Mexico, I learned what it must feel like to be the poorest person studying in a university for the rich. Dad would often forget about the tuition payments and, by the time the money arrived, so much would be lost due to miscalculations on the exchange rate that I'd have to use my own stipend to complete the fees. Since I didn't have money to squander going out and didn't even like alcohol, clubbing was out of the question. I also have the defect of believing that sex must be preceded by true love, and that didn't make me very popular with guys—or make sex-hunting guys appealing to me either…With no pretenses, no alcohol, no money, and no sex, the most obvious path to follow was that of the prodigious student. I focused my energy racking up good grades and taking extra credits. I also participated in student fairs promoting *pupusas* (El Salvador's typical dish). Years went by amidst routine, and by the time graduation was around the corner, I thought my life would remain uneventful until the end.

But everything changed *that* day…the day I received a phone call from El Salvador. What happened next made me a stronger woman, although not strong enough to say that I wouldn't have rather it never happened, even if it meant being a weaker version of myself.

My stay in la-la land was about to end.

Hamburger

Side dish:
French Fries

Common Food
In The U.S.A.

- Hamburger franchises are everywhere and offer food at reasonable prices.

Common Food
In El Salvador

- Pupusas (soft corn tortillas stuffed with a variety of pastes such as cheese, bean or pork rinds) are as common in my country as burgers are in the U.S.

- Containing about the same amount of calories, the dish depicted here has almost 1/3 the fat, no trans-fat, 1/4 the cholesterol, and 3 times more fiber than the U.S. meal shown above.

Pupusa

Side dish:
Pickled Cabbage

"You should come right now or you may never see your mother alive again."

That phrase was still ringing in my head when I hung up. As it turns out, the chain of events leading to that moment can only attest to the medical ineptitude in El Salvador.

Five years before, Mom had discovered a lump in one of her breasts. After seeking medical attention and having palpation exams from not one but *three* different doctors, she was told not to worry; it was just a fat lump. Mom knew a biopsy should have been done, but felt impotent against the opinion from the "experts" who told her everything was fine. She was given hormones instead to help her feel better. "*Ma'am this is just the menopause*"...

Two years went by and the "fat" lump continued to grow. With her concerns increasing, Mom turned to the most prominent doctor she could find in the area for a fourth opinion. The doctor ordered a mammogram which came back normal. Once again, the answer was that there was nothing to be worried about; she was only having a hypochondriacal episode.

Despite what **four** doctors had already told her, Mom could not ignore that little voice inside her head constantly repeating "something is not right, something is not right." Growing desperate, she decided to see a private doctor who agreed (finally!) to order the biopsy she requested.

Had the tumor been detected when Mom first asked for help, she could have been saved. Now it was too late.

The lump had grown tenfold and was wider than a tennis ball. Mom was immediately scheduled for surgery to remove her breast and later had several rounds of therapeutic radiation followed by chemotherapy. Although the treatment seemed to succeed in ridding her of the disease for two years, a persistent pain in her lower back later betrayed the presence of metastases. The cancer had spread.

With the same tenacity with which she had fought against the thieves breaking into our home, Mom would fight tooth and nail against her disease. She tried alternative medicine, exorcism, diet, meditation, herbs, Tai Chi, anything! She was also willing to have the most aggressive of therapies regardless of the side effects, *anything* as long as she could be cured.

In an attempt to do the most, Mom submitted to a very harsh treatment combining radiation and chemotherapy. The purpose was to attack cancer cells that had spread to her spine. Unfortunately, the treatment backfired and the intense radiation applied to kill malign cells ended up burning her internally instead. Necrotic tissue (dead flesh) gave rise to an infection which spread through her body and sent Mom into septic shock. When I received the fatal call, she was unconscious and one step away from dying.

In less than two hours I was already on my way to the airport. Soon after, I saw my Mom.

Given the severity of her condition, I was expecting to find her on a bed somewhere, with at least a nurse tending to her. Instead, she was thrown on a medical gurney in the middle of a busy hall. Alone. Her left arm hanging out in the aisle. Doctors, nurses, and all kind of people rushing through the hall often missed to see the hanging arm and ran into it. She was placed there like you place an old piece of furniture that is not useful anymore, something you just push out of the way. Nobody seemed to care. Yet that piece of meat there, that lump getting lost in the middle of the crowd, that was my Mom. The same one who taught me how to walk, spent her evenings helping me do homework, and gave meaning to the word "home" to me.

I grabbed her arm and placed it on her chest. No sooner had I done it than the arm sprang right back to where it was, it was so swollen…

The rest of the story is fuzzy in my memory. I cannot recall the details of what happened next and I wouldn't be able to continue this story if it weren't for the e-mails I wrote back then to my friends. I had transcribed portions of those e-mails for this book, but early readers of the manuscript felt the plot was too dark, graphic, and depressing to read; so I decided to save you the trouble.

When I go through the letters, I realize that nothing had prepared me for the hell I went through. Nothing had prepared me for the horrors of the medical ineptitude in my country or for the excruciating pain that cancer can bring. I also realize that, ironically, those closest to you, the ones you love most, are also the ones with the most power to hurt you.

While Mom was agonizing, I thought I could rely on my older sister. I thought we would support each other to better survive the tragedy. Instead, she left me at the mercy of her husband who treated me badly….The torment didn't last long though. Roughly seven months after I found my mother in El Salvador, she lost her battle. At that point her condition had become so bad and she was in such unbearable agony, that her death came almost as a relief. I had just turned 21 and didn't have the slightest idea of what to do next, where to go. My mother was gone. I didn't feel I could count on my sister anymore. The relationship with my father was almost nonexistent.

Because I owed it to myself—and to prove all the disbelievers wrong—I returned to Mexico and finished my engineering degree with flying colors. As a graduation gift, my father gave me a very special surprise. He kindly announced: "*from now on, don't count on me for anything else.*" I guess the guilt of abandoning a child had already been paid for by subsidizing a fancy college education, and now nobody could say that the great Mr. Campos had an illiterate daughter. Subtlety in delivering the news would have been nice, given the situation, but at least the honesty was appreciated. It was also good to know for sure that, in my planning for the future, moving with him to Panama was out of the question. Since being a single woman in El Salvador seemed too dangerous, and staying in Mexico was not too attractive either, I decided to try my luck in the U.S.A. I had no clue what I was getting myself into, but I already had my visa and what the heck! I had nothing to lose.

The good news was that the period of misery had ended at last! I had succeeded in graduating with all the honors and several specialization areas. I was armed with numerous recommendation letters from my professors and had the satisfaction of having gotten the most out of my studies. As Mom always taught me: the most valuable asset you can have, the one nobody can ever take from you, is that which you have in your head.

Having graduated from one of the finest schools in Latin America, I was ready to conquer the world! The first thing I was going to do with my industrial engineer salary was buy a nice house in a nice neighborhood, a brand new car, and lots and lots of clothes. I was going to make friends, find a boyfriend, and fall in love. I was going to go to the gym in the afternoons and eat healthy. I was going to travel and have fun. Oh! What a great life! It all made sense now, all those sleepless nights preparing for exams and term projects, all the dealing with irresponsible teammates, and with a father who didn't care enough to send money on time for trivial things such as food or rent. It was all worth it because education, no doubt, is the key that opens your path to a brighter future, allowing you to enjoy the wonders of the corporate world.

I was one in a million: smart, honest, educated, considerate, proactive, and motivated—the perfect candidate!

Note to self: it is so easy to be dumb when we're young...

A New Beginning   Chapter 4

When I relocated to the U.S., I felt very optimistic. I was under the impression that I could achieve anything I wanted here if I just worked hard enough for it—after all, everybody kept saying that, so it had to be true!

To my fortune, the same uncle who sponsored my family to come to the States, Uncle Amaro, had generously accepted me into his Virginia home. Uncle Amaro is a person who truly embodies the American dream: coming from a little town in El Salvador, he worked his tail off to become a very successful spine surgeon and businessman. At the age of 58 he had already generated enough wealth to retire and live the life. When I moved into his house, he used to spend his days enslaved to a "very busy" agenda of doing whatever he pleased. He always complained to me: "people think that being retired is easy but, don't you see? I have no rest at all! For me it is always going from a tennis match to a painting class. I barely have time to eat before attending the opera in the evenings. When it's not a piano lesson, it is the guitar. I practically work more now than before! No my dear, being retired is not easy at all."

Uncle Amaro was married to Becky, a U.S. born Caucasian woman with whom he had two kids. I was given the room at the end of the hall in their two-story house and, as soon as I had unpacked, I got busy trying to find my dream: a nice corporate job as an industrial engineer.

I had never applied for a job before, so I did what I thought I was supposed to. Besides submitting online applications on big companies' websites and checking classified ads religiously, I attended job fairs and kept my profile up-to-date on monster.com and similar websites. After submitting the first 20 applications or so, I sat tight, waiting to hear from my future employer at any minute.

A couple of weeks went by without news, but I didn't worry; I was still the cheery innocent girl fully confident about herself and her achievements. Besides, it obviously had to take some days for the human resources people to go over my application and start planning my compensation! I didn't expect any immediate answers.

…After a month of silence though…I was starting to get a *little* nervous…

I remember the full realization of my situation the day I went to a job fair and had on-site conversations with the recruiters. I was doing pretty well with my English (or so I thought) and, to spice things up, I modestly mentioned that I had graduated from *the* Monterrey Institute of Technology & Higher Education. In El Salvador, that usually produced a couple "Wooow"s or "Aaaah"s. In the U.S. all I got was a: "Where did you say again?"

At that moment the truth hit me like a bucket of cold water. The Monterrey Institute of Technology & Higher Education in this country was nothing special. All the prestige meant nothing. The whole marketing campaign saying that the university was "accredited by the Southern Association of Colleges and Schools to award bachelor's degrees" was nothing, and my years of education meant nothing. It all was nothing without a solid networking base to push me forward.

The more I think about it, the more I realize that I didn't have a chance! My curriculum vitae (of which I was so proud) was terrible! Not the content itself but the way it was written. Nobody had ever taught me how to properly make one. Add to that my not knowing a single soul working in the field, zero experience, and very bad English, and you still cannot even imagine how deep a hole in which I found myself. My uncle's family was kind to me, but they didn't know anyone who could help or guide me on this quest. It was all up to me—and I had no idea!

I lost count of how many jobs I applied for, but I do remember (and very clearly) that nothing happened. I couldn't even land a single interview. Zero. *Nada*. Five years of industrial engineering education in Latin America were only enough to get me a position as a clerk in the U.S.A., and that only because my cousin was working in the store and recommended me for it. In all honesty, I wasn't thrilled about the position, but my family emphasized that taking it would at least provide income to cover my living expenses. They had a point. I decided to take the job as a "just for now" occupation while I continued looking for better opportunities. Little did I know that "for now" sometimes can mean a very, very long time.

The Clerk

The job consisted of being a "Sales Associate" at a gift shop. On Day One, the manager of the store (an Indian lady) asked what my name was. I said: "Alejandra." She said "What?" I replied, "Al-eh-hand-ra."

"Oh no honey, that's too difficult. From now on you're gonna be Alex. OK?"

Hey! I was finally getting a job! You could call me Anita if you wanted, or Shirley. It was all the same. I gladly accepted my baptism in the "American" ways and jumped head-first into the initiation. "Alejandra Campos" the engineer, gave way to the new (improved?) "Alex" the clerk.

If I recall correctly, my salary was close to $6 per hour and I had to pay my daily bus ticket and save something for lunch. Once breaks and taxes were taken out of the check, there was not much left in it (still better than picking cotton in El Salvador though, see pg. 9).

I was able to apply my knowledge of plant planning and just-in-time production methods to efficiently accommodate mountains of greeting cards according to their category. In a way it was like being a spider. I'd spend the whole morning tidying up my web: putting the cards in place, organizing the stuffed animals per color, etc., and then I would sit in the center of it all, motionless, waiting for the preys to land ("Hello! Welcome to XYZ Gift Shop! How may I help you?"). Just like the spider, I watched my life pass me by.

The best part of my job was "cleaning day"—a monthly event in which expired candy, damaged merchandise, and all sort of treasures like those were discarded to the joy of employees who were allowed to take the waste home! It was like Christmas!!!

During the months I was an employee at the store I also had a chance to be a tourist in the city. Washington, D.C.'s downtown was my favorite part. It looked amazing. The streets, beside being clean and orderly, were filled with SUVs (sport utility vehicles) expensive enough to cover a child's education and living expenses for three years or more in my home country. There were armies of them! The overall feeling was one of abundance: huge cities, carefree wastefulness, consumerism. Even my uncle's home was equipped with a potato peeler, orange peeler, apple slicer, egg dicer—a gadget for almost every food imaginable. In El Salvador we just use a knife for all of them!

To my delight, the museums in the capital had free admission. I got to see dinosaurs, colossal diamonds, and mammoths. In visiting the museums, I discovered the subway system. It was a treat!

One day, out of the blue, I got an unexpected message from Mexico. It was good news this time. The director of my engineering department, with whom I was still in contact, was writing to tell me about an internship opportunity at a greenhouse. In his opinion, this experience would be more valuable for me than being a clerk at a store (I couldn't argue with that) and, in a matter of days, I was on my way to Massachusetts.

A City's Downtown
In The U.S.A.

A City's Downtown
In El Salvador

The Team Leader

The greenhouse I was going to work for was a very successful business. It supplied a wide variety of plants to major stores in the U.S. The internship program was highly multicultural and brought together people from countries such as Lithuania, Puerto Rico, Hungary, Mexico and, now, El Salvador. If I remember correctly, most of us were engineers. We were paid about $8 per hour to lead groups of laborers and do whatever else we were asked to.

As part of my "induction program" I had to do very educative tasks. First, I had to file piles of documents according to their dates. When I was done with that, I was allowed to perform more "engaging" activities such as dusting and cleaning closets around the office. As the summer progressed and the busy season began, I was relieved from my janitorial obligations and became a "Team Leader" instead.

Assigned to the area of merchandising, I was going to be in charge of directing and driving around a group of approximately 10 workers, mostly Mexicans. I'm not going to say they were all illegal, but they had these VERY suspicious IDs which they used in their job applications. The trick was, from what I heard, that although to the naked eye the ID was like a primary school's arts & crafts project, once you made a paper copy of it, the copy looked believable. And for the job applications, all that was needed were the copies. I guess that the employers (which I suspect were not that innocent) could always argue that it was up to the employees to provide valid documents. If any of the IDs was a fake, the applicant was the one at fault, not the employer.

This is a perfect example of an instance in which American corporations conveniently overlook the illegal status of their workers in order to profit from it. The hourly rates paid to illegal workers are often considerably less than what would have to be offered to U.S. citizens to convince them to do the same jobs under the same conditions.[26] U.S. citizens are not as desperate, plus their legal status offers them a wider variety of jobs to choose from—simple laws of supply and demand. These arrangements can produce a lot of extra ca$h for the companies.

My team and I were a happy busy bunch. Our work consisted of maintaining the greenhouse's plants once they were delivered to their point of sale. Upon our arrival to the stores, we would walk into the garden sections and proceed to water the plants, refill empty spaces, clean, etc. I remember we used to leave from the greenhouse at dawn and come back after sunset. To me the long hours were great. I was young, full of energy, and eager to save enough to buy a car. Besides, in contrast to my previous job, here I was paid for breaks and overtime. The money was coming in pretty fast.

The team leaders' supervisor, a Hispanic man, was always asking us to move faster, faster, faster! The guy would have loved to crack a whip on us. We were already working nonstop all day but he wasn't happy. One day he even asked us to stop taking our 30 minute lunch break. To me that was ridiculous, I explained to him that ours was hard work and that it would have been impossible to go 12 hours without eating. His reply was "let them eat in the car while you drive." Yeah, I thought, and when am I going to eat? His no-lunch policies were discontinued when the owners of the greenhouse heard about the situation and put an end to it.

---

26 AP, 1988. Illegal Aliens Depress Wages for Some in U.S. Available from: http://www.nytimes.com/1988/03/20/us/illegal-aliens-depress-wages-for-some-in-us.html Accessed on: 04/07/2013

I have a lot of good memories from those days. I grew familiar with the concept of driving on a highway, which scared me to death before (in El Salvador, roads were normally narrow and people drove at slower speeds). I also became an expert in carpooling "the American way."

Although driving occupied most of our summer, we had plenty of time to enjoy ourselves. When we had weekends off, we traveled to Manhattan and visited places I'd only seen in movies: the Statue of Liberty, Central Park, little Italy, the Metropolitan Museum of Art. It was all so big! So clean and nice! Did I say nice? I meant super nice!

We also had lots of fun with a group of Puerto Ricans who worked for the greenhouse. They were regularly hired throughout summer and let go at the end of the season. Rumors said that, after being fired every year, this clever group of guys would collect unemployment back in Puerto Rico while having other jobs "under the table." I never got to confirm the practice, but I did verify that these guys were really fun to be around! They organized parties where we danced, chatted, and tasted their absolutely delicious traditional cuisine. Embedded in my memory is the *Pernil Asado*, a kind of slow-roasted marinated pork. Mmm…my mouth waters by the mere thought of it! And I have to say: the notion that cooking is only for women is totally false—all the cooks there were men.

Oh! It was fun. It was nearly four months of fun, but the internship had to come to an end. When everything was said and done, I got an employment proposition which I declined. The salary offered was considerably less than what should have been paid to an industrial engineer living on the East Coast; besides, the job activities were not too attractive. I could have stayed and worked as a driver for the rest of my life, but I wasn't ready to give up on my corporate dream. Not just yet anyway.

Carpooling
In The U.S.A.

Restricted
Lane

- Special "carpooling lanes" are available. Only vehicles with two or more passengers have the right to use them.
- Carpooling decreases congestion and is environmentally friendly as it reduces the carbon emissions that would be released by driving separate vehicles.

Carpooling
In El Salvador

Passengers taking a nap

Cyclist holding on to the truck

- There are no restricted lanes to encourage carpooling and the concept itself is foreign.
- The picture here depicted is intended to represent the lack of official carpooling options.

Potential Road Kill
In The U.S.A.

Deer herds suddenly jumping on the streets and highways don't allow drivers enough time to react.

Potential Road Kill
In El Salvador

Cattle herds are slow moving but they can suddenly appear in the middle of the street after a curve or a hill. The nature of the fauna hints at a more rural condition in the region.

The Assistant Manager

After a great summer, I went back to Uncle Amaro's house and resumed job hunting. One day, while checking the newspaper ads I came across an interesting position. It read: "Assistant Manager." And here, I have to—I MUST—take a pause.

Would anyone _please_ explain to me, why on earth job titles in the U.S. are so misleading? Is the deception intentional? Or is it just a way to make employees feel better about their jobs?

For example, the title "Administrative Assistant" sounds like it entails assisting in the administration of a business. The word "administration" is directly related with the word "management," and "management" is directly related to the words "directing" and "supervising." So, why then does an administrative assistant have to constantly answer the phone for someone else and buy paper clips? How is she or he "directing" the organization by doing these tasks? Wouldn't it be better to name this position with a more understandable term such as "Secretary"? That's what we call administrative assistants in El Salvador.

In the U.S.A., a Janitor is a "Custodial Maintenance Worker," truck drivers are "Freight Relocation Specialists." The other day I saw an ad to hire "Sandwich Artists" at a sandwich shop…I didn't know that spreading mayo on bread was a form of "art." This secret code is so hard to decipher, that poor freshly-arrived immigrants (like me back then) don't even know what we're applying for!

When I read that the internationally acclaimed "ABC Pizza Store" was looking for an "Assistant Manager," I fell for it. Little did I know that my management duties were going to include answering the phone, taking the orders, folding boxes, giving out flyers door-to-door, making the pizza…I had been duped by the system.

At first I thought such dull responsibilities were a way to teach me the basics of the business before moving forward to the management aspect in the organization, but the menial tasks never ended. On the contrary, as time went by I was asked to do more. The owner of the franchise even asked me to _deliver_ pizzas when necessary. By the way, I earned more as a delivery girl than as the assistant manager!

On the positive side, the experience taught me how to manage large groups of people under the stress of rush hour when phones ring off the hook and pizzas coming out of the oven are about to fall on the floor. I also became an expert pizza maker who won timed competitions against the guys in the store. I learned that a free order of breadsticks can work wonders to defuse the tension from dissatisfied customers. And, best of all, after months of having cold leftover pizza for breakfast, lunch and dinner, I couldn't stand to see the stuff anymore!—I tried using the same approach with chocolate, but it didn't work; I'm still addicted.

After a while, it became clear that there was nothing more to the position than what I was already doing. I could have tried to save enough money for my own franchise but, with my wages, it didn't look feasible. Pizza making wasn't going to get me any closer to my dream. I had learned everything there was to learn there and it was time to go.

Unfortunately, what I saw as the logical thing to do was perceived a bit differently at home. My family seemed to be getting the impression that I had resigned from the pizza place because I was lazy and didn't want to start "from the bottom" like everyone else. Some of their comments made me feel as if they thought I wanted to live off of them and that the only reason I hadn't found a good job yet was that I didn't really want to…I sincerely think they had no idea of how hard I was trying.

Nevertheless, my relationship with Uncle Amaro had always been a precious treasure to me. He had always been there when I needed him, and I didn't want to risk ruining our friendship the same way it happened with my sister. My family had been most gracious accepting me in their home, and it was my responsibility not to overstay my welcome. It was time to leave.

I left Uncle Amaro's house the following month. I am very thankful for the time I lived under his roof and am happy he gave me the chance.

The Contractor

The U.S. can be a paradise, no question about it. I truly believe there's no limit to what you can achieve here, and for sure this is the best country I've ever seen. However, America can also find ways to chew you up and spit you out if you let it. Nobody tells you that part.

After leaving Uncle Amaro's house I felt sad and defeated. Broken inside. The American dream was not as easy as I thought. I had tried my best and failed miserably. The only thing I could think of doing was going back to El Salvador. And so I did.

The first days back in my hometown were extraordinary, full of outings and celebrations; but it didn't take much longer for me to realize that the country was deteriorating at an alarming rate. The area in which I was staying had once been blessed to have abundant water and a fresh climate, now it was a constant sauna that only got water three times per week. Things were getting expensive, criminality was twice as bad as I remembered, and my friends (all professionals) were trying to emigrate because, in their words: "there is no future here."

"What can I say?…It just didn't make sense to stay. In the U.S. I couldn't find engineering jobs, but no one guaranteed I would find any in El Salvador either. Besides, in the U.S. I could at least walk on the streets without fear of being assaulted. All things considered, I decided to give "America" another shot.

After three relaxing months in El Salvador, I packed my belongings again and returned to the land of milk and honey. The difference this time was that, for good or for bad, reality had already kicked-in and I finally understood my place in the United States. For someone like me, getting a job here meant giving up on an engineering position and considering "whatever" instead—anything as long as it was moral and could paid the bills.

When I came back to the U.S., I moved to Ohio, the same state in which my sister lived. After my Mom's death we were not the closest, but since this was the very first time I was totally on my own, it was comforting to know there was someone nearby in case of extreme emergency.

My economic situation was not too exciting. I had enough savings to subsist for six months, but I *really* had to find a job within that period or I was going to be in deep trouble. My sister was a lifesaver at the time. She had come a few years earlier to work as a physician in a medical center, and was already familiar with the area. She recommended places where I could buy groceries at the best prices, helped me get a lease on an apartment, and her husband tipped me off that a local agency was hiring interpreters to work as contractors in the area. By then, my English had improved considerably, but I still doubted my bilingual skills, so I set up to prepare like crazy for the interview. I researched and learned all the medical terminology that was needed, practiced the pronunciation as much as I could, and jumped into the water.

To make a long story short, the selection exam was not nearly as tough as I expected and I got hired!—Yay!!!

The first thing I did once I knew some income was coming my way, was to buy a used car for transportation. It wasn't only a requisite for the job but, as I discovered the hard way, an utter necessity when you live in this country. Often I've been under the impression that U.S. cities are designed assuming that the inhabitants will own a car. If you live in a suburb for example, it is practically impossible to go anywhere by foot.

I once tried walking to a grocery store, only to realize it was a terrible mistake. The problem was that although I knew exactly where the store was, the 10 blocks or so that separated it from me were major highways. Since I couldn't find any sidewalks to get to it, I took a "shortcut" through a back road instead and got totally lost. Not knowing how to go back, and without a cell phone, I kept wandering around in hopes of finding the store until the sun began to set.

As if by a magic spell, all sorts of weird guys started appearing with the darkness. A group of African Americans standing on a corner whistled at me, and a particularly obnoxious white guy in a red sports car slowly approached me and drove beside me. He was talking to me through his window and continued to offer me a "ride." I said "no" many times but the guy kept insisting (he must have thought I was a prostitute). He only left when I stopped answering his comments and kept walking without even looking at him.

On the outside I was trying to look as confident as possible, but inside I was very scared. As soon as the guy drove away, I hurried back in the direction I thought my house was and ended up in the middle of some train tracks. There were no more potential aggressors in the area, but the train could have come at any time, and it was getting darker!

To get out of there I had to jump a wire fence and, after following what seemed like car noises, I found myself right in the middle of a highway intersection cloverleaf! Luckily, I had been near that intersection before and knew my apartment building was on the other side. I just had to get to it. The highway was pretty empty and, by running as fast as I could, I was able to make it! After that experience, I understand perfectly well how deer must feel when trying to cross the roads, and I'm the most thankful woman for never having had to go through that again.

Crossing A Busy Road
In The U.S.A.

- With the exception of an occasional clueless/lost Salvadorian girl freshly arrived in the country who knows no better, people do not walk inside highways.

Crossing A Busy Road
In El Salvador

Pedestrian waiting for a
proper moment to cross

- Pedestrians are discouraged from crossing busy streets—they do it anyway.
- Note how the smoke from the bus on the left darkens the whole picture.

My first apartment in Ohio was far from being a palace; there was not much in it, but it was all mine! Since I didn't have money for furniture, I found a place that offered help to people in need like me. It was a huge warehouse with donated stuff and I could choose whatever I wanted. All I had to pay for was the delivery. So, for 40 bucks, I got myself a chair, a small table, and a nice sofa forever impregnated with cat hair (I thought I could clean it but it was impossible). The table was especially nice to have as it allowed me to stop eating on the floor, which I had never done before coming to this American paradise.

Everything was going well until the day I got robbed. I had been complaining to my building's administration about a leak in the bathroom that was turning the whole ceiling green with mold. After ignoring me for four months, the maintenance guy finally came and stole ALL of my jewelry. I'm not even talking about plastic trinkets here. These were gold and precious stone earrings, rings, and necklaces I had inherited from my Mom. Just like in El Salvador, the police came and covered everything with fingerprint dust but were never able to find the culprit—even when I knew exactly who had done it: the maintenance guy!

After the incident, I moved into a house instead. It was the house my sister and her family had lived in. She had gotten a job in a different state and had to leave, but with the housing market in the middle of a collapse, selling the property at that moment could have meant great losses. She proposed that I move into the house, paying her the same amount I was paying to rent an apartment. To me it was a win-win situation: a safer place for me and a good tenant for my sister. I happily accepted.

Work-wise, things were going well. I loved interpreting because it gave me the satisfaction of making a positive difference in the lives of people who need it the most. Working in the medical field, I helped Hispanic immigrants communicate with doctors. I did a little bit of everything: children's hospitals, OB-GYN, dental, vision, you name it. Modesty apart, I was pretty good, mainly because I was very careful and never altered what the clients said.

The extent to which a conversation can change due to a bad interpreter is scary. For example, I once witnessed a patient say something like, "Hello, my name is Marta, I know my appointment today is for a dental cleaning, but my front tooth is getting loose and I was wondering if you could take a look at that instead." To my surprise, all the interpreter said was: "This is Marta, our four o'clock [appointment]." Can you imagine that?!

Along with the satisfaction of helping others, the best part of being a contract interpreter was the "absolute flexibility" to manage my time and the freedom of being my own boss. At least that's what my employers told me when they hired me. What they didn't tell me was that contracting can be a tricky way for companies to hire full-time workers while spending as little as possible on them. Since contractors are not really employees, the company is not obligated to give them any benefits. There is no health insurance or retirement plans, and generally the company doesn't even withhold taxes or pay its share of Social Security or Medicare—which means that the contractors have to pay it all later from their own pocket.

When I asked what the procedure was to request time off, all the "flexibility" that was promised to me, was not flexible anymore. I was told that if I wanted vacations they were going to reduce my hours from 40+ per week to only "as needed."

I don't like to be taken advantage of, and since I didn't want to support such shameless cheap labor policies, I quit.

Ending my contractor days has probably been the most impulsive decision I've taken career-wise, but looking back I don't regret it. Not at all. As a matter of fact, I later found out that I was getting paid about half of what interpreters were earning in other places! What a rip off!

The Call Center Agent

I am sure I was not the first and will not be the last immigrant who accepts being a contractor without really understanding what that means, but I learned my lesson. Most importantly, I discovered that in this country the mere fact of speaking Spanish was enough to make a living, and I set up to find other opportunities in that niche.

It didn't take long to find an ad looking for bilingual agents in a call center. This time, the company hiring was a very well-known apparel chain who wanted personnel to tend to their catalog sales. Customers received the catalog by mail and called to place the orders over the phone.

Before becoming a "graduated" agent, all new recruits had to complete two weeks of training. They'd teach us how to use the equipment and how to add clients to the "no call" list (believe it or not, there is such a thing, it is not just a mythical creature—although some clients continued to receive unwanted calls despite being on the list). We were also shown the latest fashions and the "hot" items that we were supposed to promote. Scarves, gloves, jeans—the items were actually pretty cute.

The thing that surprised me about working in a call center was the incredible amount of lying that is required to thrive in the job. We were told to upsell, upsell, upsell no matter what. Whenever a client wanted to place an order, taking the order was not enough; if she wanted the orange sweater on page 14, we were supposed to say: "Oh yes, that item is gorgeous! I myself have two of those and if you look on page 26 you'll find a matching purse that is to-die-for! I got one for my mother the other day and she absolutely loves it!!!" Is your mother dead? No problem, the client won't know. Are the cashmere sweaters so incredibly expensive that there is no way you could ever afford to own them? Who cares, you can always *imagine* you do.

As part of my training I was required to sit next to experienced agents. Wow! Those guys were admirable! They could sell a brush to a bald man if necessary: the brush wasn't only for combing hair. No! It was to promote circulation and massage the scalp.

While sitting next to the agents I got to hear all sorts of conversations, the great majority from regular people interested in buying something, but there was never a shortage of weirdos, like the one that would regularly call and say "Soooo Amy…what are you wearing today?…Oh…really? Mmmm…and what color are your panties?…." The operators were already used to the guy as he called frequently. The funny thing was that, since the system was programed to distribute calls evenly among agents (nobody gets a second call until everybody else has gotten their first one), no sooner had the first agent hung up on the guy than the second agent was receiving the weirdo's call. The second agent would hang up on him again and then you'd hear the third agent say "Now I got him!" Ha ha ha! It was really funny! There was also a lonely lady who would call, not because she wanted to buy something but because she felt lonely and wanted to talk. "Yes Amy, I saw the purse on page 26, it is very pretty. I think my daughter-in-law would like it but Kate is not talking to me these days, I think it is all because Johnny has been traveling for work too much lately. They don't listen to me, I've been trying to tell them that for a marriage to work the couple needs to be together. The other day I even…"

Yeah…Being a call center agent can be a lot of fun, but the idea of lying every 15 minutes and trying to force people to buy what they don't really want or need (nor can afford) is really not my thing. I would have done a disservice to the company if I had stayed fully knowing that I hated every second of it. I decided to look for something else.

The Interpreter

It wasn't easy to find a new job this time; as a matter of fact, the weeks passed and I couldn't get anything. But providence was on my side and something wonderful happened.

Remember, I said I was a pretty good contract interpreter? Well, the clinic I had worked in when I was a contractor agreed with me. When I announced the reasons why I wouldn't continue offering my services, the staff was outraged. I don't know exactly what happened, but the group clamor reached higher levels in the company and one day, out of the blue, I received a call from a human resources representative asking me if I'd be interested to work directly for them, not as a contractor anymore. I would start working only two days per week, but the salary was better, I would have full health insurance and a 100% vested retirement plan. I loved interpreting! How could I not accept?

Going to work for the BHCE (Best Health Center Ever!) was like finding a family, everybody was SO nice to me it was unbelievable. I loved the job. I loved the people. I could not have asked for a better place. Some of my dearest friends even now are people I met there.

On a side note, although I could never complain about my job and wouldn't dream of suggesting Spanish-speaking residents of the U.S.A. be left alone and unable to communicate their very delicate health issues to doctors, the concept of having interpreters strikes me as "less than optimum" in a utopian kind of way. I guess what I'm trying to say is that it is hard for me to understand why there are efforts to offer interpreting services to the population, but there are not equally widespread initiatives to teach the language to the people. Maybe there are resources out there, but I have never heard of them, and they are not very useful if unknown.

I also don't fully understand why some Hispanics in the U.S.A. don't learn English even after extended periods residing in the country. It is such a basic need that helps us assimilate the local culture and contributes tremendously to our own good. So many doors open up just by learning the language! Without going too far, as an interpreter, I was able to support myself for about three years merely because of my bilingual skills.

I know people who have been in the country for decades and never learned English. To me this says two things: (1) The Hispanic network is so widespread and complete, that English is not indispensable. A person can live in a Hispanic neighborhood, go to Hispanic markets and work under the supervision of a bilingual boss thus never having a real need to communicate in a language other than Spanish. (2) And this I say based on my observations, sometimes a person's schedule is so busy that learning the language is not a choice. I have a friend for example, who is a waitress. She has worked five to seven days per week for the last nine years or so while constantly adjusting her plans to fit the restaurant's needs. She's been trying to learn English for a while but her unpredictable schedule makes it impossible for her to go to classes. To top it all, she has recently had her first child and is busier than ever. I hope I'm wrong, but I think it's going to be quite a while longer before she actually learns the language.

I don't want to divert from the main story too much but I leave these observations out there as food for thought.

Now, going back to my interpreting at BHCE, things were going great! I didn't make enough money to tour Europe just yet (working two days per week that is) but I had enough to cover my basic needs and plenty of time to indulge in one of my favorite activities: thrift shopping.

Thrift shopping to me equals TREASURES! It is unbelievable the quality of stuff one can find in The Salvation Army, Goodwill, and similar stores. As everything else, successful treasure hunting requires a refined set of skills and knowledge. First of all, you need to select a store located in a fancy area, where rich people get rid of out-of-season, barely-worn brand-name clothes. Second of all, you need to be p.a.t.i.e.n.t. Unlike merchandise in department stores, thrift stores don't have everything neatly arranged, you won't find the item you want in six different sizes or colors and, obviously, high quality items amount to maybe 0.5 - 1.0% of the store's goods; so be prepared to spend endless hours looking among piles of junk.

If you're not patient, forget about it; you're going to loath thrift shopping. If you are excited at the thought of finding Easter eggs hidden in the garden, or if like me, you have such a tight budget that you cannot afford any other entertainment, thrift shopping may be for you (The $10 you'd spend sitting through a movie could equal six hours walking in a thrift store and, besides the free exercise—no gym needed—you get to keep one pair of jeans, two t-shirts, and an earring set to remind you of the experience).

The Salvation Army, my favorite store back then, had special days in which certain items were half price. I think it was a Wednesday when I decided to wake up early and go as soon as the store opened so that I could finally get my hands on that black Banana Republic blazer (tag still on!) I had been eying for a while. The price was a whopping $12, but that day with the discount I could get it for $6. It was still kind of high for my limited budget, but the piece was so beautifully made that I had to have it.

I woke up, took a shower, and hurried to the store. When I arrived I couldn't find the jacket anywhere; after a thorough search of the racks, it became evident that it was gone. It must have made someone else very happy... and that was fine. I had a comfortable feeling of relief knowing that I hadn't been able to spend the money I knew I couldn't afford anyway, I looked around for a few hours and finally left with the satisfaction that I could have gotten any item I liked in store—because I didn't like any.

When I arrived home I was welcomed by a surprise. Can you imagine what it was?

If your thought was that somebody had broken in through the kitchen and stolen every single valuable item I owned, you are clairvoyant for that is what I found. This was the second time things were stolen from my residence in less than a year. *Come on!* I was the person paying $40 for a donated sofa full of cat hair! Why did people keep on stealing from me? I had nothing already!!!

This time, when the police came and started dusting things, I already knew what to expect (nothing). I was a pro in the art of getting robbed.

I was starting to see a pattern of crime here and it was scary for me to think what could have happened had I been there that morning. The robbers had to have been men, strong enough to kick the back door open. Their moral character must have been dubious at best, and nobody would have heard me screaming had I been caught off-guard while sleeping in my bed. What a horrible thought!

I became terrified of living there alone. I would have taken on a roommate but, previously, when I was unemployed and asked my sister about it she told me that she and her husband would require a payment of $200 for every $300 I made out of a sublease. They said they'd use the money to create an emergency fund to fix any damages the roommates could cause and I'm sure that made sense to them, but it certainly didn't make sense to me. Since bringing in company was out of the question, I moved out. If the mountain won't come to Muhammad, Muhammad must go to the mountain.

The Roommate

My experiences living with strangers have been memorable to say the least. Thanks to them, I've gained a better understanding of how undocumented immigrants must feel when they try to save money by living in overcrowded conditions, several families cramped under the same roof.

The very first time I had a roommate was a DISASTER! I found a girl online who turned out to be a guy in real life and had the most disgusting hygienic habits. Living with this person, I had to get used to having car tires on top of the kitchen table, dirty dishes stored in the cupboards, and puddles of an unidentified yellow liquid around the toilet (Ewww!). The bathroom in our house was covered with "dust" particles that regenerated overnight every time I cleaned them. The brownish particles were everywhere, on <u>every</u> surface, and—upon closer examination—they turned out to be *skin* flakes! I didn't last too long in there…

My second roommate experience fared a little better than the first one, but I would like to make an emphasis on the word "little."

This time, I moved into the house of a Hispanic woman who also rented her attic to a Hispanic guy. The decoration inside the house included an impressive palette of greens: from the walls to the sofa, to the tiles in the bathroom, to the kitchen's stains. My room was also green and, although small, it had a glass sliding-door leading to the garden which doubled as window and let the sunshine in. I was happy in my little nook.

If it had been up to me, the common areas in the house would have been a lot tidier, but after a failed attempt at modifying my previous roommate's hygienic habits, I had learned that **the only person you can change is yourself** and so I limited my worries to the realm of my room.

What I didn't foresee was the influence of Micho, the cat. This animal was a hybrid between a household pet and a wild feline, a tangled ball of orange hairs that roamed the streets all day and spent the nights sleeping at home. I think Micho liked me, because he used to poop in front of my door. He also loved to pick quarrels with other cats in the neighborhood and was often wounded during the fights. More than once, I had to remove his dusty scabs from the table cloth before eating, but that wasn't the problem. The problem was that Micho was infested with fleas.

As long as the cat was in the house, sleeping on the floor, the bugs would easily and readily feed from him; but when my landlady gave birth to her first baby and decided to get rid of the cat, the insects had to find other mammals to feed on. Can you guess who the lucky ones were?

From one night to the next the house was infested. You'd walk on the carpet and fleas would jump at your ankles to bite you. They were really hungry! At first I naively thought that keeping my bedroom door closed was going to keep the pests out, but in my desperation to keep an extra clean environment I ended up bringing the bugs in. You see, I didn't know that when you vacuum a flea-full carpet, the little animals get *in* the bag and stay there until someone else (*moi*) uses the vacuum cleaner in another room and pretty much sprays them out.[27] The more I cleaned the carpet, the more the bugs came in. Their numbers increased so much that I became afraid of walking in my room. In the evenings, when I came back from work, I ran my way through the living room, check my legs up to the knees and, once the absence of fleas was confirmed, I'd jump on my bed and stay there. Eventually...all my attempts were futile...there were fleas *everywhere* and no place was left to hide. We tried smoke "bombs" against the bugs, powders on the carpet, you name it, but the fleas wouldn't budge.

As if the fleas were not enough, my landlady announced that her boyfriend was going to move in with us and the young man in the attic was also considering bringing a friend. So now it was going to be the owner of the house, her boyfriend, the other tenant with his friend, the baby, the fleas and myself. The house was turning into a *meson*.

The same way people in the U.S. think of famine in Africa (a very sad, unfortunate event that is happening far, far away from us; a well-known story we wish we could do something about but rarely do) is how middle class Salvadorians think of the less privileged classes living in *mesones*.

---

27 There are scientific studies reporting that the trauma inflicted by being vacuumed would actually kill the fleas, but I am pretty sure some of them survived in **our** vacuum cleaner (which was not in the best shape) and then came out.

A meson is a kind of collective housing, a substandard boarding house in which people live piled up on top of each other often without the basic needs of a modern home. These places frequently have whole families living inside one room and are equipped with a single bathroom/kitchen that all the families must share.[28]

How likely do you think you are of ending in a place like that? Probably as likely as I thought I was (not likely at all!). Yet, contrary to all prognostics, I opened my eyes one day and found myself right there, living in an "American-style" *meson*.

It is interesting how our existence can change so radically from one moment to another. You may be used to waking up every morning, drinking your coffee and going to work, blissfully numbed by the relative comfort and predictability in your life; but the truth is that despite the false sense of stability, you have **no** guarantees. Nobody ensures you won't be laid off tomorrow. There is no way to know if a drunken driver will kill your family tonight. You are constantly exposed to a lottery of events (out of your control) that could potentially change your plans.

As a teenager, I believed that if I just kept on being a good person and applied myself to my studies, destiny would somehow reward me with the proverbial work+family+house trinity. Never did I expect that my first job out of college was going to be that of an underpaid clerk or that I would end up dusting some stranger's butt-flakes off the toilet seat.

You better start appreciating what you have now, even if you are 10 pounds away from your ideal weight or don't have enough money to buy that brand-new SUV just yet. Make the most of your blessings while you have them because they are not yours to keep, they are merely a temporary loan that may last you the next 60 years or the next 60 days, there's no way to know.

***

Struggling to make ends meet and renting a room in a dirty house infested with fleas, I had reached rock bottom…

…Yet sometimes, when you are sinking, reaching the bottom is the only way to propel yourself back up…

---

28 Murcia de López, Elizabeth; Castillo, Luis, 1997. El Salvador: a case of urban renovation and rehabilitation of mesones, *Environment and Urbanization v.9. n.2.* p 161–183. London.

Playing By The Book

Chapter 5

"All right. It is time to lay the cards on the table and think. What can I do to get myself out of this dirty ditch?

First of all I need to increase my income, what are my choices? I could try pole dancing, I hear the pay is good and I'm already equipped with all the assets. Mm…no, who am I fooling? I could never stand objectifying myself like that or enduring the lustful guys, let's think of something more in line with my morals. Oh! What about becoming an egg donor! That would help a struggling couple and could easily rack me some major money. I've seen ads offering as much as 10K for popping a few pills, having a few injections, and a minor surgery. Hmm…but what about the side effects? My Mom died of breast cancer, who knows what those hormones could do to me. Besides, if I get in the hands of a butcher, I could end up worse than I started. No, it doesn't sound like a good choice. I need something more sustainable in the long term…"

Sadly but truly that was my train of thought back then. Some of the things I considered seem clearly unacceptable to me now, but I wanted to mention them here so that you get an idea of what being desperate really looks like. Suddenly, a whole lot of options start crossing through your mind; options you wouldn't normally think of if you weren't in need. That's why, when I hear of someone doing a reprehensible act, I try to hold my judgments and first understand what led the person to do that. It doesn't mean I will condone the act, but I will strive for understanding instead of basking in empty criticism.

After evaluating the many ways in which I could increase my income, I reluctantly decided to use the most profitable part of my female body. Why deny it? It was simply the most logical thing to do and I'm not afraid to admit it. Ain't no shame ladies; if you're blessed with it, work it! I highly recommend it: use your brains!

The truth is that at some level I always knew that furthering my studies (going for a master's on top of my engineering degree) *had* to be a way to open more doors for me. Uncle Amaro had been hammering the idea into my mind for quite some time, yet I refused to listen. Or you could say I listened, but I was so skeptical about the idea (five years of engineering didn't really get me much), and so unwilling to relive that period of deprivation, that I adamantly strived to find other ways to move forward without having to study again.

Uncle Amaro was not the only one trying to convince me to go back to school, there was also this pesky little voice inside my head. Call it subconscious, Holy Spirit, or schizophrenic hallucinations but there was something inside me constantly asking:

"Alex, when are you going to apply to grad school?"

"Alex, shouldn't you be preparing to take the admission tests?"

The nagging was easily ignored at first, but as time went by and the quality of my life sank faster than the Titanic, the volume of the little voice grew louder.

It wasn't until I found myself in a dirty, messy, flea-infested house that I finally understood. It finally hit me. Things weren't heading in the right direction and it was time to do something about it. What the hell was I thinking when I let myself fall so low?!

With newly found resolve, I went to the public library, borrowed a "Graduate Record Examination" (GRE) self-prep book and sat at my desk with the firm intention to study for the admission tests. No more than thirty seconds had passed when the phone rang. The person calling was a patient I had interpreted for at a clinic six months ago. Back when we met, Elena had casually inquired where I lived. When I told her that I leased a room, she said, "If I ever buy a house, would you consider renting a room from me?" Being open to the idea, I gave her my phone number but hadn't heard from her. I had totally forgotten about it when I got her call.

Now, this is the part that gives me the chills. To me it feels as if God had been talking to me all that time. He was telling me to study, study, go to grad school, apply, but I refused to comply. The more I resisted the worse my life became; and then, as soon as I started doing what I knew I had to do, as soon as I opened that book, the phone rang to give me a way out of the flea nest I was trapped in. Would you say that was a coincidence?

Elena's house turned out to be amazing. The spacious property she lived in had previously served as a model-home for a recently built development and Elena had gotten to keep all the fancy furniture and decorations. It was a brand new unit and a 180° turn compared with my little green room. Do I even have to say it? I happily moved on the spot. Bye bye Micho! Bye bye fleas!

Elena's family was incredibly nice to me. Her partner Jose Conde, her teenage daughter Bivian, and her toddler Maribel—they all welcomed me warmly into their home.

Every member of this family had enough personality to fill a reality show; especially Bivian, with her love for makeup, long straight hair, and sexy attire. In the evenings, after coming back from school, she would blast reggaeton music on YouTube and twerk[29] like a professional. You should have seen her! She learned dance steps from videos and reproduced them to the dot. Her family was used to this and with time it became normal to me too, but I must confess her legendary upside-down-booty-shake-against-the-wall never stopped amazing me.

All of Bivian's dancing did not distract me one bit from my more pressing goal: getting into grad school. The more I learned about the process, the more I understood that simply applying was not enough. I had to *wow* the admission committee *and* get a full scholarship if I was going to make it. The tuition costs were simply too high for me to afford. There was always the choice of getting a loan but—knowing that a professional degree is not a guarantee of employment—I was not willing to take that risk. Broke and in debt? No, thank you!

---

29 To dance sexually, shaking one's butt with abandon and grinding against your partner.

The application process for me was a pain and I won't bore you with the details, but when everything was said and done there were reasons to celebrate: not only had I been accepted to a master's program, I had also been awarded *two* different graduate fellowships that would cover my entire education and living expenses as a student in The Ohio State University (Ohio State). I could not believe my luck!!! An overwhelming feeling came over me, one of hope, of possibilities…I have no words to explain.

Although the news was great and I felt elated, there was also a little catch…if I accepted the offer, I had to commit to being a full time student, dedicate 100% of my time to the program, and that meant quitting interpreting. Oh man! That was a difficult choice! Interpreting at BHCE was a dream job. After years in the position I still enjoyed every moment I spent with the patients and the warm relationship I shared with the staff. Besides, I had been out of school for so long that my brain was rusty. What if I didn't make the cut? What If I wasn't good enough? In order to maintain the financial support I had to produce good grades. What if they kicked me out and I ended up unemployed?

Endless fears roamed inside my head, almost to the point of paralysis. It is so dang hard to get out of your comfort zone!…Still, I had to acknowledge that my current position had no room for growth; staying would have meant settling for a "blah" existence and embracing stagnation. Shouldn't we humans aim for more? I let go of my fears and jumped into the unknown. Again.

The Waitress

Classes did not start immediately. University rules stated that I had to wait for the next autumn quarter to begin, which was great for me. Why? Because after doing the calculations it turned out my stipend was going to be *less* than what I made interpreting three days per week, and things being as they were, I could not afford to get any closer to the poverty line.

Like a little squirrel gathers nuts before winter, I had to save as much cash as possible before I wasn't allowed to work anymore. For that purpose I took a couple of extra jobs, the first of which was as a waitress.

If I could transmit one take-home message on behalf of all the waitresses in the world, it would be to ask diners to leave a good tip—would you? I know the economy is bad and all, but if you can afford it (and if you're eating out, most likely you can), it wouldn't hurt to leave an extra dollar or two. Waiters' paychecks in the U.S. are ridiculously low, and the servers must rely almost entirely on tips to make a living.

Living out of tips is not necessarily a bad thing though, some of the girls I worked with would easily pocket $100 cash on a single night. But I guess not all of us are so lucky (or skilled). I personally was terrible; waitressing was definitely not my forte. One day a customer said: "I would like one sixty-three please" and I wrote a very clear "63" on the slip. When I returned with the order she asked "Are you sure these are the *Chimichangas*?" And I, totally oblivious as to what that thing on the plate was (to me they all looked the same) said "Hmmm…This is the #63 that you ordered."

"But I ordered one sixty-three" she said. And I had no idea why she was repeating what I had just told her "Yes ma'am, this is one 63." "Nooooo!" she said "I ordered OneSixtyThree! As in one hundred sixty three!!" Ohhhhh!... Oops...

The restaurant I worked in was fully staffed with Hispanics in the kitchen. I had a lot of fun with the guys, but was profoundly saddened by witnessing the American Dream being truncated again and again.

Here is what happened: Most of the guys came with the intention to stay a few years, work hard to support their families and earn enough money to build a house in their countries. They didn't really want to remain in the U.S.A. forever; the plan was to become financially stable and then go back to their loved ones. BUT, once they found themselves being discriminated against, living in overcrowded conditions (e.g. eight guys in a two bedroom apartment with one bathroom) yet totally alone and isolated (*sorry sir, no speako the English*), they seemingly became so depressed that they forgot their purpose. Alcohol and drugs became their best friends and they started spending most of their income on these fleeting distractions. The result was that they ended up breaking their backs, working like slaves to move forward, but never managed to save enough to reach their dreams.

Besides drugs and alcohol, guys found another very expensive distraction: women. Did they forget they had a wife and children in their own countries? Where was their loyalty? In their attempt to escape loneliness if only for a night, many became unintentionally laden with multiple families, and with the burden of providing for them all.

I honestly don't understand this, my little brain simply cannot find a logical explanation. If you are already broke and in a precarious condition at best, why on earth would you not care about bringing more children to this world? They are an added expense, an added responsibility and require a lot of care. I cannot even presume it's done to obtain tax deductions, because I've met people who declare as many as eight imaginary children on their tax forms and get away with it.

Oh my, people...I don't understand you sometimes...

Working at the restaurant was a good experience overall. If I have children, they will have to go through this too, so that they can learn the true value of money ($8 is more than a ticket to a movie, it can also represent one hour out of somebody's life) while developing respect and consideration for others regardless of their economic class. The people serving you have the same feelings you do, please be considerate.

The Temp

Waitressing was a good source of income and free food, but it was not good enough; I had to look for something else. A friend of mine mentioned having an acquaintance that was willing to pay me *$20,000* in exchange for an arranged marriage. By then I had already fulfilled the requirements to become naturalized (e.g. five years as a green card holder, 18 years of age or older, etc.) and, having received my citizenship, I could have granted my "husband" a legal status if we married. But the whole scheme was so fishy and risky that I graciously declined the offer. Guess I wasn't that crazy after all.

To complement my income I became a "Temp" instead. A guy I knew worked at a temporary staffing company and helped me get a weekend job in a donut factory. When I heard the news, images of Willy Wonka came dancing to my head. Delicious donuts with caramel filling, chocolate glaze, and strawberry jam were sitting there just waiting to be eaten. They must have felt so lonely, I was gonna take them out of their misery!

To be a part of "XYZ Staffing Services" people had to report to the main office at 5 o'clock in the morning. After passing a drug test and IF there were any openings, applicants were sent out on assignments right away. Otherwise, they were welcomed to "try again tomorrow."

Since I had inside connections, I was able to avoid all that hassle and reported directly to the plant instead. The trip was more like a family outing since both Bivian and Jose accompanied me; they were temps too. Upon our arrival we were assigned to different tasks and didn't see each other until lunch time, when we'd happily drive to the neighborhood's Chinese restaurant and gobble up all the beef-broccoli we could before our 30 minute break was over.

Although I thought I would hang out with the lonely donuts, they were nowhere to be found ☹. Instead, I had to suit up in protective gear and work with acids strong enough to eat through my skin on contact. My task consisted of cleaning gigantic kettles and stainless-steel surfaces that were covered by an unknown gooey substance. It was probably a mixture of flour, dust, sugar, and humidity that had been aging for centuries in the most forgotten crevices of the plant.

NOTE TO SELF: money paid for 1 plate of broccoli beef = 1 hour of my life spent scrubbing brown goo back then. Do not forget. Don't forget where you come from and don't forget what you've been through.

One thing I should mention about my experience as a Temp, is my surprise at the noticeable harassment I got from the guys; not only from my Latin co-workers, but the Hispanic supervisor employed by the plant as well. They were all quick to shower me with compliments, profess their never ending love, etc. etc. The interesting thing was that the same supervisor who profusely flirted with me, did not utter a single word to female Caucasian (legal, English speaking) engineers who oversaw the plant…Caucasian supervisors did not harass me either; it was only the Hispanic ones. I think this says something about our Latin culture.

In our countries—or at least in El Salvador for sure—flirting with women is the most normal thing for guys to do, and girls are used to it. Men jokingly use slightly sexual or suggestive references in virtually any setting—at the office, the university, everywhere. It is not out of place because nearly everybody does it. But when it happened at the plant it was striking because, after so many years living in the U.S.A., I was used to being treated with more respect.

On several occasions I was teamed up with a guy whose name I can't remember. He was a chubby white Mexican, with a mustache, short curly hair, and a rather handsome semblance. As I said, I don't remember his name, but that is irrelevant because he liked to be called "Cachimbon," sort of a weird name but he loved it.

Cachimbon was a flirt, he did not discriminate. Regardless of age or size, any woman would have been welcomed into his arms. I still remember one day he was trying to convince me that we were the perfect couple because we cleaned the tanks faster than everyone else. With an utmost cheerful attitude he told me:

"¡Cuando trabajo solo soy chingon, pero juntos somos dinamita pura!"

This is hard to translate but means something like "When I work alone I'm awesome, but together we're pure dynamite!"

The phrase struck me and stayed with me for all these years because I couldn't believe anybody could have been so excited, so happy and motivated while cleaning a dirty tank in a factory. It brought about an epiphany in all senses of the word. I had a sudden realization of what the situation meant for me and what it meant for him. He probably felt the luckiest person for having landed a $10 per hour job. He was likely very happy to make such generous wages (compared to wages in our home countries) and was hoping to keep things going that way. I, on the contrary, saw the experience as a necessary "evil" to move forward onto something else that was already lined up for me, by me.

And here's where you realize what the power of the mind really is. I know it sounds like rubbish but think about it: how can you go forward if you have no intention of moving? If my priority is to *remain* a member of the cleaning crew, what are my chances of becoming the CEO? Nobody is going to force me to change if I don't want to. It seems logical that we're more likely to achieve great things if we set our *own* goals high to begin with, doesn't it?

Please don't get me wrong here. I'm not implying there's something bad with being a member of a cleaning crew—that is a perfectly respectable occupation and I myself was doing it. I'm also not saying that a person in this position can't decide later on that he would like to be the company's CEO. All I'm saying is that you have to want something to happen before it does, simply because it is you who has to make it happen!

After Cachimbon and I finished cleaning the whole plant, I was moved to "quality control" (yet another case of inflated work titles). *There* they were those sneaky donuts at last!

My super important job consisted of grabbing a stick and watching the pastries moving on a conveyor belt. If any donut was broken or damaged, I had to push it off the belt with my wand. And that was it. Hold the stick and push. Hold the stick and push. Hour after hour after hour...The minutes seemed sooooo loooong...

On one occasion I ventured to take a bite out of a rejected apple fritter. The pastry looked delicious but as soon as I tasted it, my fantasies of gluttony were shattered. As luck would have it, the factory only cooked products half way and the donuts were raw. The glazes I had imagined in all the possible flavors weren't even used there; they were added at the point of sale and everything in the plant tasted horrible. It was a huge disappointment, but it saved me from gaining at least five pounds and getting some clogged arteries in the process.

And that was my life back then. There isn't anything else to say. Months went by and I kept on holding my three jobs while saving as much as I could until college started.

The Grad Student

Since I've always loved food, I chose to pursue a Master in "Food Science and Technology." When I chose the program, I was following a train of thought which was very similar to the one that got me in the donut factory. Yes, I wanted to learn all about the food industry, I also wanted to expand my knowledge of food formulation and manufacturing. But more than anything, I was excited about all the delicious food I would be able to work with!—for some reason food always gets the best of me.

Going to graduate school marked a new beginning. Instead of living in small rented rooms, I decided to move closer to campus and have my own apartment. To furnish my new home on a very limited budget, I shopped around for key items on CRAIGSLIST® and complemented the pieces with treasures taken out of "select" dumpsters (only from rich neighborhoods). I used these materials and my sense of style to decorate the place and the results were remarkable! From the white futon in the living room to the hand-made wall art, it all looked very polished. I received tons of compliments on it!

When the final touches were done, I sat in the living room and went through my mental list: Home, check ✓. Furniture, check ✓. Hopes and dreams, check ✓. I was ready!

My first day of class was unforgettable. To kick the year off we were having a food analysis lab. The teaching assistant (TA) who guided the class gave a brief welcome and went on to say:

"Today we will be titrating sodium carbonate with hydrochloric acid. You'll measure aliquots of NaCO3 into beakers and then you'll use your pipette to add the designated solvent…"

He continued explaining what we were going to do and I felt I was being spoken to in Chinese. Burette, pipette, titrate, beaker, conical flask, aliquot…I had never heard those words in my life!

With a background in industrial engineering, I was trained in things like optimization, plant planning, management, and quality control. Titration was not very high in the list of priorities. To make matters worse, even when I had used some of the items before, I had never been instructed on their English names. Food science was truly a foreign language to me.

After the TA finished explaining the scope of the lab, he announced: "Now we're going to have a small quiz on what I just explained." I almost died. My fear of not measuring up and ending unemployed came back to me and I wanted to cry; but that wasn't the right time, it was time to take the test. As best I could, I answered the five quiz questions and turned them in. Don't ask me how (because I have no idea) but when the grades were returned, I had obtained an A!

Common sense and logical deduction helped me dodge the bullet that time, but no amount of acumen by itself was going to keep me afloat for the next two years. I had to do something else.

The first thing I did (like any logical, mature grad student would do) was to cry nonstop. I didn't consciously want to; the tears just came out of their own will. Many people think of weeping as a sign of weakness or sadness, but I beg to differ in opinion. Based on what I've experienced, tears are merely a sign of intense emotion; be it anger, surprise, frustration, despair, happiness, you name it. In my case, those tears were pure fear.

For the first week or so, whenever a new acquaintance said: "Nice to meet you! How are you liking grad school?" I would start answering but, by the time my mouth had uttered the second word, my eyes were already pouring. Sobbing would then set in and I wouldn't even be able to speak. How embarrassing! Not only for me, but also for the stranger who didn't see that coming and had to end up consoling me and patting me on the back while saying: "Don't worry Alex, it will be OK. I promise, it will all be OK."

The good thing about being so lost is that you have nowhere to go but up. My old interpreting job had already been given to someone else and I was not about to end up unemployed without at least putting up a fight—you haven't seen me fighting yet.

Once the initial shock was over, I got to work. Whenever a weird term came my way, I carefully wrote it down and made sure to look for its meaning after classes; most of the time, the definition of a weird word involved yet more weird words, which resulted in an exponential cascade of weird words increasing without control.

When "Organic Chemistry for Dummies" just didn't cut it anymore, I asked my TA to recommend a better reference book. The guy was an angel. He told me that most of the concepts I was looking for were not really in text books. According to him, those were things people learned while taking food-related undergraduate courses which were not in my background. The TA then kindly offered to personally explain all my questions during his weekly tutoring hours.

Poor soul, he didn't know what he was getting into. For the next month I made sure to visit him weekly, loaded with a long list of doubts and topics. We'd spend hours together at a time, and I'd only leave when everything was clarified. I'd swear that, by the end of that period, I could perceive a slight spark of anguish in his eyes every time he saw me near his cubicle.

I knew my constant cries for help put me at risk of seeming incompetent. Previous experience had taught me the politically incorrect truth that, when it comes to learning in the U.S., there can be a prejudice against people who don't look white, especially in the presence of a strong foreign accent. White people have a "learning curve" when they make a mistake or don't understand something they are learning. When Hispanics make a mistake they're just dumb. Fortunately, I had no time to worry about appearances or senseless ideas like that; all my energy had to be focused on getting up to speed.

And I did it! After two months of intensive preparation, the emotional breakdown passed and things didn't seem so daunting anymore; I became just as competent as everyone else. I cannot say the rest of the master's program was easy, for it truly required a lot of effort, but from that point forward I never doubted my ability to succeed.

...Do You Speak Mexican?

As a grad student in the U.S.A., I felt like I finally fit in. Compared to the penniless days in Mexico when all my classmates spent money like it grew on trees and I remained forever the party pooper (Alex can't come with us to Cancun. Alex cannot afford dining at the hottest restaurant. No, Alex does not have a car to drive to the event), at Ohio State all my friends were just as broke as me.

We understood the joys of half-price sushi Tuesdays, the value of "buy one, get one free," and the incredibly persuasive power of free pizza. Together, we would engage in low cost activities such as hiking and playing board games. We would also frequent outdoor festivals full of art, freebies, and street performances.

A Street Performer
In The U.S.A.

- Creative form of public entertainment.
- A team of back up dancers and modern stereo equipment supported this juggler's act.
- Tips were welcomed.

A Street Performer
In El Salvador

- Last resource of beggars or drug addicts.
- No additional team or equipment.
- Stationed at street intersections, performers take advantage of red lights to request money from drivers. The interaction can sometimes turn violent if tips are not provided e.g. verbal attacks or banging on the windshield.

I made great friendships at Ohio State, not only with U.S. citizens but also with Turks, Indians, Ecuadorians, Chinese, Thai, Africans, and Peruvians to name a few. I learned a great deal from all of them and continued to expand my knowledge of different cultures and religions in the process.

Professors were top-notch, absolute eminences in their areas of specialization who also cared about the students. My advisor was amazing and never doubted my capacity. There was also Dr. Perrot, my statistics teacher—a man as quick with his mind as he was with his words. He was a joy to talk with!

Among all the knowledge and brains, there was one thing that took me by surprise. It was not something new, I had experienced it *ad nauseam* before, but I never thought I'd find it at the college level...

For some reason, wherever I go in the U.S.A., somebody *always* comes up with the legendary question. **Drums please**

"Do you speak Mexican?"

Oh my gosh...Where to start with this question...

I should begin by saying that I understand its source. When I came to the U.S. and was exposed to a variety of ethnicities I wasn't familiar with, every member in a particular group looked eerily similar to the others, and at times it was hard for me to tell them apart.

This is not a racist statement but rather a well-documented phenomenon known as the "other-race effect." It explains that humans are less likely to remember a face from a racial group different from their own.[30] I guess that when a group of people look very different from us, it is easier to remember their similarities than their differences. If one day you walk across a group of 10 women with blue skin and orange hair, you are more likely to remember these traits instead of the curvature of their eyebrows or the shape of their lips.

So, I understand. I understand that we Hispanics as a group may "all look the same," but for goodness sake I'll try to set the record straight—hopefully once and for all: although Mexicans are likely to be one of the Hispanic groups with the highest rates of migration into the U.S.A. (given their "advantageous" geographical location) the term "Hispanic immigrant" is not a synonym of "Mexican." I repeat, the term "Hispanic immigrant" is *not* a synonym of "Mexican." This statement has nothing to do with the qualities of being Mexican and is merely based on the fact that Latin America comprises many other countries besides Mexico.

I have nothing against Mexico. After living there for years and having worked alongside Mexicans in the U.S.A., I know they can be very warm, kind, smart, successful and determined people. I love my Mexican friends to death! But if I tell you that I come from El Salvador, please realize that I'm not too likely to speak "Mexican." To the best of my knowledge such a thing does not even exist!

---

30 Sangrigoli, S., Pallier, C., Argenti, A. M., Ventureyra, V. A. G., & De Schonen, S., 2005. Reversibility of the other-race effect in face recognition during childhood. *Psychological Science, 16(6)*, 440-444.

As far as I know, most Latin countries speak **Spanish**. Each place may have its own colloquialisms (e.g. "Pisto" in El Salvador means "Money" while in Mexico it means "Booze" —this created confusion when I complained that "my father has not sent me my pisto yet") but overall, it is Spanish for most of us.

Phew! Now that this tidbit is off my chest I can continue.

The Truth

Yes, we Hispanics may all look alike, but I think we're very different. Without going too far, based on the age of arrival in the U.S., I'd say there are three kinds of us. Those who were born here and those who came in their childhood are very lucky, because they had the chance to better assimilate the culture and immerse themselves in the language from a younger age. The third group though, the one I belong to, is a little more clueless about the "American ways" because we came here as adults and all we grew up knowing was the way things work in our home countries, which is VERY different to say the least.

At times, Hispanic friends of mine who belong to the first two groups don't fully understand the struggles of immigrating later in life. They don't fully grasp that many of the roadblocks we clueless adult immigrants face upon our arrival are simply a result of ignorance, a consequence of basic pieces of information that we just don't know. It is like opening a combination lock. Opening the lock in itself is really easy and shouldn't take you more than a few seconds *if* you know the combination, of course.

How I wish life came with a manual! My youth would have been so much simpler if I knew then what I know now. Don't you wish life came with a manual? Maybe we can start building one? Here are two tidbits of wisdom we can start with…

Truth No. 1: Career Counseling—the truth that came too late.

If I could go back in time and help my 21-year-old-self when she arrived into this country, the first thing I'd do would be to tell her about the existence of "career counselors." These people make a living out of helping others develop their careers and are a great place to start when you are clueless. The best ones are those affiliated with universities as opposed to freelancers who may be more interested in your money than in you.

When I was about to graduate with my master's I worked with career coaches to improve the structure of my résumé, understand what happens during interviews, and be prepared to answer tricky questions. Additionally, they debunked the mistaken notions I had on what works and what doesn't when you want to get employed.

After talking to them my eyes were opened. No wonder I had gone from industrial engineer to pizza girl! I had been doing all the wrong things! Here is what they told me:

"Newspaper ads, job fairs and internet postings are all a farce. Ads are meant to be 'cattle calls' when all that is needed are bodies to fill irrelevant positions with no skill requirements. The objective of job fairs is to make money for the hotels and publicity for the companies. Delivering your résumé directly to a company's headquarters is the 'beggar's way' and they practically throw the papers away as soon as you turn your back. Applying online means submitting an application among another 500-2000 people and since there's normally only one screener to choose the two or three that will obtain an interview, they come up with random filters, such as 'today I will only read the résumés which have the name on the top right corner' and they discard the rest. Statistics* show that 85% of the people who find a corporate job do it through the 'unknown market' i.e. through connections and networking."

So, until you create your own network of friends and professional contacts, you are highly unlikely to get a good job. This is particularly important when you are an immigrant in the U.S.A. who knows nobody. Keep in mind that enrolling into a respectable college is a good way to start building relationships with faculty, recruiting agents and fellow classmates who will eventually become employed. It also helps "revalidate" your undergraduate education if you have one. Once you earn a U.S. master's degree, companies start believing that you in fact have a valid bachelor's degree.

Truth No. 2: Defense Exams.

Thanks to Dr. Perrot, my statistics professor, this second truth did not come too late. It came just in time to give me peace of mind before my college career's final examination. Knowing my perfectionist nature, I would have agonized for months in anticipation of the test if it wasn't for his wise words. Here is what he said:

"Defense exams go one of three ways. **Way #1**: there is a problem with the thesis. Then 99% of the time the defense is postponed. **Way #2**: the thesis is 'rubber-stamped.' Questions are asked, but the answer can be found in the thesis itself. Either the thesis was truly exceptional (not often), or the committee had other things to do before the defense and nobody really read it in detail except (maybe) the advisor. **Way #3**: at least one committee member has decided to 'humble' the student one last time before graduation. So, hard questions are asked until…the student cannot answer and feels humiliated. The approach to take in this case can be either (1) fight and claw back as long as you can—knowing that in the end you probably will not know the answer; or (2) use the politician's technique of bullshitting and stalling—saying lots of words that don't really mean something. Example: 'your question is very much in line with a comment by such and such in paper bla-bla…' If you are good at this, you can use up to 5 minutes…Another approach is just to state: 'I don't know, because this is not where I have concentrated my efforts. But here is how I would proceed to find an answer to your question. The textbook by Chiquita® Banana is a classic reference for…'

"I have served on gazillions of defense committees. Anytime there has been a problem was simply because the student built it up as a huge mountain, got extremely nervous, and went into complete panic. You are composed and talented. So don't worry. **There is no way that you can know the answers to all the questions.** Other committee members often do not know the answers to questions asked by one person. So we just act serious and behave as if all of this is well known and trivial. We scribble some idiotic stuff on a pad of paper while our minds are saying 'Thank goodness I don't have to answer THAT question…'"

---

*That is what a career counselor told me. Although I don't know his sources, I believe he's right.

Dr. Perrot was absolutely right—as usual. By the time the evaluation committee members allowed me to defend my thesis, all the hard work had already been done. After endless days working on my research I couldn't help but memorize every single detail about it. I was ready.

My final exam did not take long and soon after, the professors were shaking my hand and congratulating me on my work.

As for that girl who started the program crying in the halls and didn't know the meaning of the word "aliquot," she had gotten straight As in all of her classes. There was a hideous "A minus" intruding her perfect record but she handled it.

She had made it! She had officially become a Master of Science in the U.S.A. *Cheers!*

Chapter 6   Corporate America

If I had to describe it, I'd say that corporate America is like the popular rich kid you met in high school: loved by some, hated by others, respected by all. He had the coolest clothes, a fancy car, and was the captain of the football team. All the girls wanted to date him.

Mr. Popular did not hang out with everyone though, he was actually very picky. To be accepted in his group you had to prove you were the right fit. You had to prove your personality matched his taste and your skills served his purposes. Who do you think he'd have preferred? The outgoing cheerleader who had mastered all the backflips or the rude troublemaker who only knew how to pick her nose?

Many were the kids who wanted to join Mr. Popular's ranks but few were the chosen. Those who made it to the other side found their efforts rewarded with higher social status, elite life events, and *safety*—the safety of knowing that as long as they were "in" they would be protected by the group.

…But, as you know, nothing in life is free. To keep getting all these benefits, those who hang out with Mr. Popular have to remember one thing: Mr. Popular *is* the boss. He isn't their best friend. He has expectations from all of them and they better keep up.

Remaining in Mr. Popular's good graces often means making him your priority, attending endless meetings you'd rather avoid, and doing what he asks you to do even when it doesn't seem logical—all just a small price to pay for the joys of belonging.

In my case, it took a long time for Mr. P. to notice me. I had flirted with him for years but he always ignored my advances. Only when I completed my master's degree did I become attractive enough.

My diploma was just a little paper, but it held all the power needed to convince the system that I did have something good to offer and that my capabilities reached beyond the realm of physical labor: I was also well suited to *think*.

With a U.S. master's diploma in my hands I was in a whole other league. Employers wanted to talk to me at last, and I interviewed with many companies. The selection process was lengthy and nerve-racking and I made all the possible mistakes you can think of ("No sir, I would never like to work for company X, I've heard they're intern slavers. Oh…your company is a branch of X…well, actually, when I use the term 'slaver' what I really mean is…"). In the end, I didn't get a job offer, but I did land an internship.

The Intern

Internships are great opportunities for professional newbies to gain experience in their areas. They serve as a win-win arrangement between companies and future job-seekers, because companies get qualified cheap labor to support their permanent staff, while interns get to have *something* to put on their résumés—there's nothing worse than the feeling you get fresh out of college when there's absolutely nothing to put on that dang paper!

A good internship has many advantages when done properly, that is, when the intern is assigned meaningful tasks. Companies can train and "test-drive" prospective employees for several months and, if things don't work out, they can easily say "thank you and so long."

As far as interns are concerned, the opportunity means getting hands-on training while getting paid for it, a once-in-a-life-time chance to hone soft-skills before stepping into the real world, and the perfect occasion to find out if the work environment and location of a particular company is in line with their expectations. As an added plus, young professionals with some sort of internship experience are more attractive candidates for jobs than those without.

Lo and behold! After I successfully completed several rounds as an intern, the job offers started pouring in! It had taken me seven years, but I was finally getting a glimpse of my American Dream. I had run in the middle of highways, been robbed a couple times, shared my bed with fleas, and cleaned up donut factories; but I was now going to be a part of Corporate America. Hallelujah!

The Product Developer

The company I chose to work for was an international giant, a leader in its field. The potential for growth within the organization was practically limitless and I loved their office atmosphere. I sincerely thought that I had found what I'd been looking for so long and I promised myself that I would do my best to keep them happy. It had taken a lot of work to get me there and I was going to make the most out of this wonderful opportunity.

My official corporate title was "Senior Associate Food Technologist" and I was the person in charge of creating those "new and improved" food products that consumers get to see every month in their grocery stores. It may sound easy in theory but it is trickier than you'd think, especially when you consider that every company has an intricate system of rules, protocols and regulations that must be followed while developing a product. At the end of the day though, the pride and satisfaction a product developer gets when her new "baby" hits the shelves is totally worth the effort.

The monetary aspect was not bad either. My paycheck was average for the position but, if you compare it with what I got at the donut factory, you could say I was in the seventh heaven. For the first time in my life, I had enough money to buy pre-washed lettuce in the supermarkets and $6 lattes without remorse.

It was so easy to embrace the abundance! Going to Walmart was not a source of stress anymore; it became my favorite hobby! I just filled up the carts with everything I wanted and never worried about the bill. I even bought my share of unnecessary kitchen gadgets, like the automatic iced tea maker I never used, the onion chopper that didn't chop, and the microwave egg poacher that mysteriously disappeared from its drawer.

And my 12-year-old-second-hand-twice-crashed car? Did I ever mention all the headaches it gave me? Driving it on the snow was like being pulled by drunken reindeer! I replaced it with a brand new crossover vehicle that was a joy to take to the carwash. It looked so shiny!

More than shopping sprees and carwashes, more than trips around the world, the one thing I loved the most about my corporate life was the people. I had *the best* team a person could ever wish for. We all understood each other and worked harmoniously toward our department's goals. I was confident about the products I developed and was getting good feedback from my boss.

If I was discriminated against for being Hispanic, I never noticed it. Every single aspect in my existence was in order; the future looked promising and, in short, I loved my life!

Woman Carrying A Heavy Load In The U.S.A.

Coming out of a grocery store.

Cloth is used to cushion/ stabilize ⇐

Woman Carrying A Heavy Load In El Salvador

Coming from a public outdoor market.

A Carwash
In The U.S.A.

The car goes to the carwash.

A Carwash
In El Salvador

"Carwasher" guy negotiating price with car owner ⇨

The carwash goes to the car.

The Numbers

How I wish I could end this book right now. I'd love this to be the story of a clueless Latin girl who migrated to the States, overcame adversity, and reached her corporate dreams. Wouldn't that be nice? This point right here would be the perfect ending! I am tempted to stop…But I can't! There are still four more chapters that need to be told!

What happened???…That is a question I still ask myself: what happened? Everything was going so well at the office, how could things possibly have gone wrong? Do you really want to know? Well…let's just say that a little gremlin escaped from the dark dungeons of co-worker-land and came into my life to haunt me.

As much as I wish I could, I cannot give you the details. But I am guessing that if you've worked in group settings for a good part of your life, you must have come across one of these gremlins at least once (they are attracted to large groups of people) and you will understand: just like a rotten egg added to an otherwise delicious quiche, a single gremlin is enough to alter a whole department's operation. The dynamics of this phenomenon are actually fascinating.

Although I can't tell you the details of what transpired, I can tell you that, almost overnight, things got really complicated. Normally, to reach a 4, I simply added 2 + 2. But now, reaching 4 looked more like solving the following equation:

$$x = \frac{\frac{3595}{5} - 6! + \sqrt{(48/2(9+3)) - 45 + (23*6/3)}}{933^2 - 870{,}485}$$

Does it look complicated, vague, or plain wrong? Well, welcome to my world!

At one point I found myself working as much as 14 hours a day chasing what seemed like moving targets. It was so frustrating! The job I once looked forward to so eagerly became a life-long sentence and I felt miserable all the time. I'd go home after 10 hours of stressful work just to find that I couldn't sleep thinking how to dodge the knives the next day; and then, when I finally fell asleep, all I had were nightmares.

I started having euphoric episodes on Fridays at 4 p.m. (5 is almost here!) which were only surpassed by the deep sorrow of Sunday evenings. I would stay up reading, writing, surfing the internet on Sundays until 1 or 2 a.m. in an effort to extend the weekend as long as possible. It was indeed a sad feeling to close my eyes knowing that as soon as I opened them again, it was going to be the dreaded Monday, and the cycle of frustration would start once more.

The only way I was able to make it through the day was by anesthetizing myself with food. Whenever I felt frustrated (which was often) I'd grab a donut or muffin to calm the nerves. I gained 8 pounds in four months and none of my pants would button anymore. Eventually, I had to buy new ones because the risk of having a "wardrobe malfunction" in the office was getting too high.

Besides the clear message my growing derriere was giving me, that pesky little voice I knew so well (the same one who nagged me to the point of exhaustion until I applied to grad school) had returned with a vengeance. Now, the voice constantly harassed me saying things like:

"Alex, what are you doing here?"

"Are you sure you want to spend the rest of your days in this cubicle?"

"Alex, come on! There has to be more to life than this!"

I knew by experience that little Miss Pesky Voice should not be ignored. I had to at least listen to her comments and evaluate her concerns; otherwise it was impossible to get her to shut up. As a good industrial engineer, I resolved to do a cost-benefit analysis on the situation. I took a calculator and did a "Percentage Enjoyable Life Analysis" to find out if the corporate world was really good for me. I decided to rely on numbers (which never lie unless you make them) to give me an unbiased estimation of the *quality time* my cubicle life produced. I know there are many other things one should evaluate, such as medical insurance, retirement plan, etc., but I decided to analyze time because in my opinion it is *the* most important commodity a person can have and the only one that can never be recovered or replaced. On the next page, you will see what I found:

Alex's Percentage Enjoyable Life Analysis

	Day	%
+ Days in a year	365	100
− Working days (52 weeks/year * 5 working days/week)	260	71

Please note mornings are spent preparing to go to the office.
Office hours often extend until 6 or 7 p.m., there are 30 to
60+ minutes commuting to and from work and by the time you are done
cooking, eating dinner and washing the dishes, there is barely enough
time for you to wash your face, check e-mails and collapse into bed.
Thus meaningful living time during weekdays is negligible.

	Day	%
+ Vacation days (15 days + ~10 holidays)	25	7
Gross livable life:	**130 days**	**36%**
− Daily Maintenance (12 h/day out of 130 days gross livable life)	65	18

As with any other manufacturing machine (and most employees are
machines either producing thoughts or goods to make someone else richer
—the most advanced, easily programmable machines I must add...), you cannot
run humans non-stop, that would be risking breakage and undesirable down
time; humans also need a certain degree of maintenance in order to keep
producing. On a daily basis humans need to sleep and eat as minimum
requirements in order to function properly. Estimated sleep needed for a
"comfortable, enjoyable" life: 8 h (for all of you new mothers and dads, grad
students and resident doctors, I am aware you are sleeping less, but you tell me,
is this really a desirable, comfortable life?). Cooking two meals: 1h, eating 2
meals: 1 h, third meal will come in the form of a candy bar, doughnut and coffee,
pizza, or similar ready-to-eat concoction that will minimize machine down time.
Miscellaneous (unclogging bathroom, going through mail, finding the cat, etc.):
1 h. For the sake of our fellow humans, let's include 1 h for shower, hair,
make-up and dressing up (I am being positive here, I know several women who
need 1 h just for hair).

	Day	%
− Weekly maintenance (0.5 -1.5 day/week. Average: 1 day/week)	52	14

A weekly, more in-depth care is generally recommended although not
necessarily required. Instead of deep cleaning and oiling a machine's gears,
human weekly maintenance involves: grocery shopping, laundry, cleaning the
house, ironing office clothing, balancing the check book, preparing food in
advance, etc. which easily takes your whole Saturday afternoon, especially
if you have the luxury of staying late in bed that day. Note: Add children to
the equation for at least 1 less day per week to account driving to and from
sport events, music lessons, helping with homework, tantrums, etc.

	Day	%
Net enjoyable life:	**13 days**	**4%**

I couldn't believe it! The results were worse than I suspected.

As you can see, when we feel trapped within the "corporate rat-race," we have less than 4% of our entire adult time to live and do the things we actually enjoy doing[31]. We'll dutifully continue to be so for at least 30 or 40 years until the human gear mechanism becomes so worn off with carpal tunnel, arthritis, obesity, vision loss, etc. (in other words, until our throughput becomes so unacceptable) that the only thing left for our companies to do is to "retire" us, replace us with a new model. We are then "free" to leave with an insufficient social security check or, for the lucky ones that are able to save an additional money-cushion, to do whatever we feel like doing—which at the age of 70 or 75 could very well be staying at home and waiting peacefully for our deaths.

Oh! But death is not a problem! Not at all. Because part of the master plan is to ensure that the human resources are not only self-maintained and trained, but self-renewable. After all, it is not in vain that we work so hard; no, we do it so that *our children* can have a proper education and a proper future as our replacement in the new generations of corporate human machines.

It is beautiful indeed! From an engineering perspective, humans are the best resource to work with!

When I understood these cold facts, I became sort of depressed…I felt that I had been mentally programed since childhood to look for the end of the rainbow but, once I found it, there was no pot of gold. The dream I had been chasing for so long (the idea of being a successful corporate woman) and the decades I had already spent on that pursuit, they all had been in vain because, to me, the corporate world sucked.

When I say it sucked I don't mean trivial issues with troublesome gremlins; I mean it from a broader perspective, from the "meaning of life" perspective if you will. Why are we in this world? Are we really supposed to spend our days confined in a cubicle? Are we using this ephemeral life of ours to the best of our ability? Where are we going to be if we continue doing what we're doing right now? Is that where we really want to be?

For some people, being part of the corporate world can be a wonder. I've seen fellows who truly seem to enjoy the meetings and the paperwork, and that is absolutely GREAT! They have found their place in life and are already spending most of their time doing what they enjoy. Good for them! To me however, cubicle America was not the best choice. When I examined the purpose of my existence, I realized that being there was definitely not it, and if I continued on the same path for another 10 years I would inevitably turn into a single 40-year-old lady, with three cats and a very biter attitude.

I had come to a fork in the road. I could continue living for the brief vacation periods that I earned by working my 8 to 5 job, and ensure myself a very comfortable future 40 years from now; or I could take 30 years' worth of vacation time in advance and use that time to try to find a more meaningful existence for me *right now.*

---

31 The actual number is closer to 3.56%. This calculation does not apply if you truly enjoy what you do in the office.

Considering I had good savings, no children, and outstanding frugal abilities; I was in a perfect position to try. I could even sell my car if need be. The more I crunched the numbers the more I realized that I could in fact survive on my own for a while. I was young, healthy (knock on wood), smart, and willing. I had also dug myself out of deeper ditches before—when I was broke and didn't even speak English correctly. I was now in a much better position to dig myself out again if I needed to. Why wait?

The idea of quitting started fluttering in my mind. It is not that I couldn't continue. Actually, in a bipolar twist, the source of all my problems had come under control and things were getting back to normal; harmony was returning to our office and, best of all, the products I was developing were getting rave reviews. I had absolute certainty that, if I remained in the position, I would slowly but surely climb my way up to the top...but *I didn't want to!* It did not make sense to me anymore! I wanted more from life and I had to get out of there to find it.

The path I would choose next would be decisive for my future. The more I thought about it the clearer things became. But, once the decision was made...Would I regret it? Or would I just wonder why it took me so long to take the leap?

Leap Of Faith   Chapter 7

"The truth is that our finest moments are most likely to occur when we are feeling deeply uncomfortable, unhappy, or unfulfilled. For it is only in such moments, propelled by our discomfort, that we are likely to step out of our ruts and start searching for different ways or truer answers."—M. Scott Peck

When we were children, how many of us imagined we would become what we are now? How many of us thought: "When I grow up I want to be an employee. I want to wake up every day at 6 a.m., get ready for work and drive half an hour to my office. Then, I want to dwell in a cubicle from 8 a.m. to 6 p.m. without getting paid overtime, solving someone else's problems, and making someone else rich. I want to make sure, of course, that I spend the 10 hours at the office sitting nonstop on a chair, typing words into a computer and eating donuts until my butt grows to impressive dimensions and my eyesight starts failing me (that way I can make use of my vision insurance—if I have it—to buy a pair of glasses and look cool). Having carpal tunnel would be a nice plus, and lots of meetings! Yes! How can I forget the meetings? I want endless hours of delicious confinement within cozy conference rooms, discussing the same topics over and over until my tongue runs dry. Hopefully, I'll be bossed around by someone with no idea of what s/he wants, and I'll get to restart my projects continuously from zero according to some daily whim. That will be *da bomb*! I love unnecessary work! Wow…this is so exciting! I can't wait to grow up!!!"

How many of us had different plans? And when did our dreams die? Did they die when we got our first loan to pay? Or did they die after our first 10 job rejections because we didn't have enough experience?

Didn't we want to be exciting things? Like rock stars, astronauts and super heroes? When did we let our dreams go? Why?

Gathering The Courage

As days passed by in my cubicle I continued to grow dissatisfied with the outlook of my life. Sometimes I'd walk into the office before sunrise and leave after sunset, spending entire weeks in a continuum of darkness. I felt like the proverbial canary trapped inside a golden cage. While singing for its masters, the bird will never starve or die frozen in the winter, but it will never fly free either.

I wanted to leave, take a risk and find "my calling" but…how do you find it? Does it even exist? The security of a corporate job was a tangible reality, how could I abandon it without concrete evidence of a better future out there?

The most logical thing to do was to look objectively at my choices. I could stay or I could leave, that part was easy to deduce. Now, what would be the worst that could happen in both scenarios? If I stayed, the worst that could happen would be the gradual withering of my soul and the realization of having made a terrible mistake once it was too late. If by the time I retired at 71, I was a bitter lady with no life or desire to live, there would be absolutely no way to get my life back. My time on this earth would have been utterly and categorically used up and the only thing left for me to do would be to "deal with it." Hmm...and what would be the worst that could happen if I left? Well, I could easily waste two of the best years of my life chasing deluded dreams of grandeur, end up broke, unemployed, and haunted by a suspiciously long period of inactivity in my résumé which would be difficult to explain to prospective future employers. All of these outcomes would be very uncomfortable, no doubt, but would they be irreversible? Would I be condemned to forever stay like that? Mmm...no, not really. After working in Corporate America for a while, I had rediscovered myself and validated my abilities, I believed that most companies out there could benefit from my skills and there wasn't a compelling reason why I wouldn't get hired in the future if I wanted to. Besides, having years of professional experience and good recommendations, I could apply to a better position in a smaller company and maybe even relocate to a better town. When I looked at it that way, the decision to leave seemed less daunting.

After analyzing the "worsts" I also had to look at the "bests" (good things can also happen). What would be the best outcomes for each scenario? If I stayed, I could become the head of the company in 20 or 30 years, adjust my schedule to meet the organization's needs and live happily ever after with my millions. Still, as long as I remained an employee, my salary would be purposely calculated to be less than what I actually generated for the company—you know that, right? If a corporation starts paying its employees exactly what they are worth, there would be no profits and the company would collapse; it just wouldn't be viable. On the other hand, if I went on to become a successful entrepreneur and generated millions with my own ideas or products, I could eventually sell my company or license my inventions to live on the royalties. There would be the potential to earn a considerable amount of money while freeing my time to do whatever I pleased. One thing that Corporate America had taught me was that developing products which yield millions in profits is far from being rocket science. It is not easy, I grant you that, but there are thousands of average people out there doing it successfully. I could not see any reason why, if I put my mind to it, I could not be as successful as the "Spanx lady" who went from selling fax machines door to door, to being one of the most renowned self-made billionaires featured in *Forbes* magazine by the age of 41. Yes, I know this is a far stretch (no pun intended), but we're talking about the best case scenarios here.

In any case, the most obvious conclusion I could draw from my observations was that my chances of succeeding at finding a fulfilling life were better if I quit than if I continued spending 96% of my time absorbed in activities which were not conducive to what I wanted.

I have no way to explain it, I had no guarantee that I would do better, no indication that in this time of economic crisis I was even going to be able to find a job later if I needed it. The only thing I knew was that I wasn't going to be happy staying there. I wanted to at least try a different route and I couldn't keep on postponing the decision forever. I had to act soon; better yet, I had to act *now*, because "now" may not be the best time to do things, but it is the only time we have. "Yesterday" and "Tomorrow" are only intangible ideas.

In the end I gained the bravery to quit only when I considered the city that I lived in. My company's headquarters were located in a very small town in the middle of nowhere. The town's main attractions were the local bar and a

Walmart and, besides my work, there was nothing there for me. I concluded that a life like that was meaningless and I preferred to die than to live another 40 years of it. In short, I wanted a life worth living: if my life wasn't worth it, I didn't want to live it.

In my depressed state, committing suicide seemed like a viable option. But I didn't want to take the "easy" way out just yet. So I made a plan: before doing anything else, I would take one last shot at finding a fulfilling existence. Should I fail, should I end up in a homeless nightmare collecting cans from dumpsters, then I would kill myself—and I would have the peace of mind of at least having tried.

As wrong as this premise may be, once death becomes the only alternative, being courageous suddenly seems easy in comparison.

Jumping

It took me three months to make up my mind and conceive the notion of quitting as a doable feat. I personally think this was a very short time considering that quitting meant letting go of all the preconceptions I had about what life was supposed to be and who I was as a person, all of those ideas that had been placed inside my head (and I accepted as truths) since a very young age: *"Thou shalt be born, grow, get a good job, and die"*—with a family, a house, and a dog somewhere in between—that's what I was programmed to believe.

From the time I made the decision to the day I actually quit there were at least four more weeks. Changing one's life is not easy people!!! Walking into your boss' office and uttering the words is a piece of cake, at the most it takes five minutes and 40 calories; but gathering the valor…now *that* is the hard part! There's a mental battle taking place inside you, with heavy emotional armor and nuclear explosions full of "wouldas, couldas, shouldas" spinning out of control in anticipation of all the possible outcomes. It can all be summed up in one word: FEAR. We fear the unknown and fear change; this emotion can have immeasurable power on us but, fortunately, it can only go as far as we let it.

Although I reeked of fear, I knew that taking action was the best medicine to cure the condition. So, one good day in April, I armed myself with courage and walked into my boss's office for a one-on-one. The time had come. I wasn't sure if I was going to change my mind at the last minute; after all, I could always pretend to myself that my plans of leaving had all just been a big bluff. It would have been very easy to stay mum during the meeting and return, unharmed, to the comfortable but boring stability of my cubicle.

I think what eventually made the difference in my resolve was that I had rehearsed, word by word, what I was going to say. Once I started my speech there was no turning back…In a matter of one hour I had given my resignation and, to my surprise, my amazing boss had taken it pretty well! He said he understood my personal reasons and, even better, he would gladly be a reference for me should I ever wish to return to the corporate world.

Suddenly it was all over. It was just a memory, like the day I learned how to ride a bike, the day my mother died, and the day I left El Salvador. It had just been another event, the normal beginning of a new stage in this unpredictable life.

As reality sank in, something strange happened. For the first time in a long time, I started looking forward to the future. Mondays were not dreaded anymore!

Interestingly, when word spread that I was leaving the company, all my colleagues turned out to be surprisingly supportive. Not a single person thought I was making the wrong choice, which still kind of puzzles me since I was blatantly choosing unemployment. Maybe they thought I was dumb but chose not to tell me out of politeness (?); I guess I will never know. The word I heard the most over the following weeks was "Congratulations" which I cannot understand either because to me, given the circumstances, it was like congratulating the mourner during a funeral. Still, at least four people approached me in confidence and declared they envied me immensely and would do the same "if it wasn't for the mortgage, the car, the children…"

At a point I felt like the *estandarte* (standard bearer) of the free soul, as if I had a responsibility to succeed in my pursuit of freedom in order to show my fellow cubicle dwellers that there is a way out.

Not everybody was supportive though…Uncle Amaro was very clear in his disappointment. He spoke to me like emitting a sentence. He said: "It will take one or two years to find out the virtue of your decision [an open ended phrase which guarantees an 'I told you' in the future regardless of the outcome] as it took a year and a half to find out that not taking the job with the other company[32] was a mistake [Ouch! Besides emphasizing perceived past mistakes, this is like saying 'you will eventually *fail* again']." So demoralizing…I hadn't even started doing what I wanted to do and the predictions from my dearest family member were those of defeat. But that's fine. I think my uncle was merely concerned about my future and believed (correctly) that Corporate America was the safest bet for my well-being. At the end of the day though—and this is something we all should know—the life you are living is *yours* and yours only. It is wise to hear advice from family and friends but, ultimately, it is you who should make the crucial decisions—because it will be *you* dealing with the consequences later…

My last days in the office were incredible; I was overwhelmed by the extent to which my coworkers went out of their way to show their affection. Everyone, from the maintenance team to the highest executives, had words of encouragement for me. Every so often, while I worked in my cubicle finalizing pending tasks, friends would drop by unannounced and shower me with advice, hugs, flowers, heartfelt goodbye-letters, lunch invitations, Girl Scout cookies, chocolates…What can I say? I was immensely lucky!

---

32 When I decided to accept my current corporate job, I had to reject another position with a great company located in the trendiest area of a big city. Uncle Amaro thought the rejected opportunity would have been an overall better choice for me considering everything the city had to offer to young people.

My wonderful immediate team also organized farewell get-togethers with coffee, cake, and many presents. The guys even gave me a Walmart gift card anticipating my imminent bankruptcy. They said it would help me "when you don't have money for groceries anymore." But the guys were wrong, the card didn't last that long. In less than a month the funds were gone. Actually, I had my last "guilt-free" shopping spree with it, complete with shiitake mushrooms, pre-washed lettuce, and $6 lattes! Thank you guys!!!

The greeting card (cover and inside messages) my immediate team gave me as a farewell on my last day of employment.

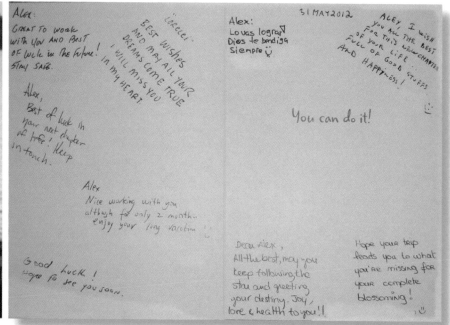

Moving On

Thursday, May 31st was my last day at the office. By 6:00 p.m. I had cleaned out my desk, returned my badge to the administration, and left the corporate-road without stopping to look back. I slowly walked out of the building carrying all my personal belongings in two boxes. I'd swear that with every step I took the air seemed cleaner, the sun brighter, and the colors more vivid. I felt happy, liberated.

You, my dear reader, must know that by the time I signed my resignation, I had already thought carefully about what I'd do during my sabbatical. I wasn't leaving Corporate America just because I didn't like it. I was leaving because I wanted to do something else. I had a plan. This plan wasn't easy to conceive for it required getting to the root of what I truly wanted to accomplish with the time given to me on this earth, and *so much* of what we strive for can be based on pure brainwashing! I, for instance, had spent 30 years blindly doing what I thought I had to do, in order to become someone I thought I was expected to be, even when I didn't have a particular vocation to be such a person.

While searching for my "true longings" I discovered that the best source to turn to, the less corrupted by society's conventionalisms, is the little kid inside us. Besides being the most honest, this source is also free because ALL of us were children at some point. Back when we were little, we all had dreams, true dreams—the kind that aren't discarded based on profitability (or lack thereof) and are not intimidated by the many reasons why "it wouldn't work."

Let's take a look at a boy who wants to grow up and become a dragon slayer for example. When he makes his choice, he isn't thinking about the average salary for the position. He isn't concerned by the prospect of finding dragons to slay either, all he knows is that the idea excites him and he'd love to do that for a living. Now, of course I'm not proposing to throw all common sense out the window, not all of us can grow up to become princesses and astronauts. But if you remember being fascinated with the idea of rescuing damsels in distress from the wrath of wicked dragons, is there any way you could translate that *inspiration* into a feasible adult livelihood? What is it that you really liked about the dragon slayer? If it was helping people in need, would you find the same satisfaction being, say, a paramedic? What about a firefighter? Would working for a company that furthers human rights be a better fit? There are so many choices. And once you focus in on something that tickles your fancy you just have to figure out what you need to do to get there. You should also make the necessary calculations to ensure you're aiming at a position with an income level adequate for your needs (e.g. if you like human health, do you need to earn a brain surgeon's salary? or would you be fine with a lower paying position like a medical aid?) Keep in mind that sometimes a small income doing something you really love can give more happiness than twice the amount earned from doing something you loath. Also, before making any decisions, talk with someone who is already doing what interests you to truly understand what the position entails. The last thing you want to do is spend years and money becoming a dental hygienist just to find out that you're grossed out by people's blood, tartar, and other unnamable oral "surprises."

As for me, there are two things I remember wanting to be when I was a child. First, I wanted to be a secretary. I had no idea what a secretary did but I do recall being excited at the idea of clicking the keys on a typewriter. From that standpoint you can say I succeeded, as I typed words in my corporate cubicle the same way a hamster runs in its wheel. The second thing I wanted to be was a millionaire. Again, I did not know how anybody became a millionaire, but I wanted to have tons of money like Rich McDuck so that I could be the owner of my time, eat lots of candy, and travel around the world.

Looking back it occurs to me that what I really wanted wasn't simply to type on a typewriter, I wanted to write. I wanted to bring stories to life and preserve them for posterity on a piece of paper. It then occurred to me that maybe, just maybe, writing a book would also help me move closer to the second goal.

I knew that having a book published would be a long and painful process (as is often the case when we want to accomplish something big on a topic we're not familiar with) but, again, it occurred to me that there was nothing stopping me from trying but myself. The only thing that was for sure was that I'd never achieve anything if I didn't attempt it.

Let me put it this way, in the big scheme of things: we, our souls, our self-awareness, all that stuff, can either be eternal or end with death. If everything ends with death, our time is too short not to try achieving what we want (if all you have is 50 years of adulthood, do you really want to spend them all doing something you don't enjoy?). On the other hand, if we are eternal, even a lifetime of misery (should your plans fail) is nothing but a blink in the grand scheme of things, so why not risk it and take a chance?

Unlike self-help books out there, which are written by folks who have already succeeded in achieving their goals, I am just starting. So, technically, I have no grounds to guarantee that anything I'm saying will work for you, or even for me. In a sense this is a leap of faith, I'm basically proposing that we jump into an abyss with the firm conviction that "the gods" will save us before reaching the bottom and, honestly, I don't blame you if you're skeptical. But here's what I'll do: since I believe there's so much to be gained from this experiment in terms of our quality of life, I am willing to jump first. I'll test the waters sparing you the risk, and then I'll tell you if it works.

…Actually, come to think of it, if you're reading a published version of this book and you're not my friend or family member, chances are that at least I survived the fall!

Chapter 8   Long Forgotten

One difference between legal and illegal immigrants is the amount of traveling each group can do. Illegal immigrants think twice before leaving the country and often have to miss their daughter's wedding, father's funeral, etc., because they know very well that, once they step over the border, there's a real chance they'll never come back. The costs to return illegally can be too high and the risks grow increasingly unbearable. As a result, there are many Hispanics in the U.S. who consciously decide not to see their families and homelands for extended periods of time as long as they can continue "enjoying" the American dream. Then, when they finally return to their countries, something curious happens: the place they remember is no longer the same. Life back home has gone on without them.

Although I have been lucky to visit San Salvador with some frequency, every time I go the city seems a little changed. First there were a few new buildings and streets I was not familiar with, then the restaurants and coffee shops I used to like weren't open anymore. Lately, even my friends are not quite what they used to be; many have migrated out of the country in search of a better life, while others have gotten married and are way too busy with their children to go out together the way we did before.

Interestingly, even the things that have *not* changed in El Salvador seem out of place to me now. I guess that after so many years living in North America I've gotten used to a 1st world country lifestyle where pollution, noise, and urine-smelling sidewalks are no longer the norm. It's so easy to get used to the good stuff! But once you are accustomed to higher standards, going back to subprime levels is kinda tough.

When I quit my corporate job, the first thing I did was to take a couple weeks' vacation in San Salvador. Previously, when I went into "unemployed mode" my budget was restricted to the most basic needs and traveling was not an option. This particular trip, however, had been planned several months in advance and was under zealous supervision by my all-time best friend who had chosen me as the maid of honor for her wedding. Yolanda would have *killed* me if I had cancelled on her at the last minute! Besides, a tropical getaway like this was perfect to recharge my batteries in anticipation of the uncertain life I was about to face. I packed my bags without delay.

The Coach Class

I've been traveling by air for as long as I can remember, and all I have to say is that the service has deteriorated considerably. When I was little, flying was an exciting experience that I looked forward to. Flight attendants treated you like royalty—even in coach class—and meals were feasts with delicious desserts that looked more like works of art than food. Getting through airport security did not require you to get naked (well, almost naked) and nobody was x-raying your private parts.

When it was time to get into the plane, children and First Class may have gone first, but nowadays the list is interminable. I don't even stand in line anymore. First I patiently remain seated while the Diamond, Platinum, Gold, Silver, Presidential, Premium, Premium Plus, Premier, Executive, First and Business class passengers board the aircraft; then, I continue waiting for those who paid extra to get priority seating. By the time I get in with the regular mortals, all the overhead compartments are full and there's no space left for my carry-on.

The rest of the trip seems to have morphed into a psychological torture. The last time I flew to El Salvador, the airplane's cabin was cold like a freezer but blankets were "reserved" for the elite 1st class only. Passenger leg room was small enough to cause claustrophobic attacks. There was no free food whatsoever (not even peanuts or pretzels) but the crew tempted hungry passengers by offering good-smelling snacks at "reasonable" prices.

The deterioration that air travel has seen in recent years is justified. There are dangerous security threats now that didn't exist before, fuel prices have sky rocketed and, ultimately, the public is the one who made the call by choosing cheaper fares at the cost of lousy service. Still, I firmly believe that all airline CEOs should be required, as part of their duties, to fly overseas in economy class at least once per year and have a limit on the use of private jets. The executives look very nice on the airplane's screens when they appear on cutesy promotional videos at take-off telling us how "important" we are, but that doesn't keep me from freezing while flying over the Atlantic. They've forgotten that their customers are the ones ultimately funding their paychecks.

So, I say: get the CEOs to feel the pain! And then watch how conditions improve on the airlines.

The Insecurity

Landing into Comalapa International Airport (the most important Salvadorian airport) always gives me good chills. For some reason I am always incredibly happy when I get off the plane. Originally, I was excited because I knew my Mom was waiting for me on the other side of the glass door; but now, even when no one is waiting there to hug me, I continue to feel the same anticipation and eagerness to walk out and submerge myself into the country.

My best friend's future husband was supposed to pick me up from the airport this time but, as usual in our Latin culture, he was late. So, I sat outside on the sidewalk and contemplated what was happening all around me. The first thing I noticed was the warmth, not only the 88°F temperature but the evident warmth and friendliness from the people. I would have gladly stayed there for hours imagining the story behind every familiar Hispanic face that anxiously looked for its *hermano lejano*[33] among the travelers coming through the exit door. I could almost feel the emotion of the mothers standing next to me, bursting into tears at the sight of their children; the grandmothers who could barely walk but rushed limping through the crowd to hug the newly arrived. I saw men crying; young men covered in tattoos who, despite their tough exterior, could not hide their emotions any longer. As soon as they were safe in their family's arms they had license to be vulnerable again, and they cried. I wondered what all they had been through to feel that way.

---

33 "far away brother" see page 11

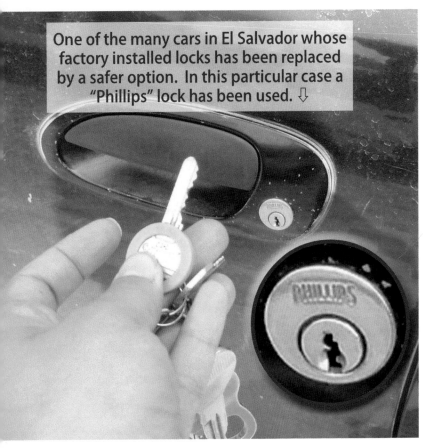

One of the many cars in El Salvador whose factory installed locks has been replaced by a safer option. In this particular case a "Phillips" lock has been used. ⇩

I was taken out of my thoughts when my ride arrived. The groom-to-be apologized for the delay and helped me take my luggage to the car. As we walked, I felt I was in the idealized world from my childhood memories, a place that once gave me everything I needed and kept me safe. But the illusion did not last long, as soon as we reached the parking lot I started to remember…

My friend's car was there waiting for us. We loaded the luggage into the trunk and walked towards the front seats to start our drive back to the city. I didn't notice anything out of the ordinary until I raised my hand to open the door…something was off.

Like many cars in El Salvador, my friend's had been vandalized. One day when Yolanda's grandfather was visiting some acquaintances, thieves forced the original locks open and stole the car's contents. By the time Don Juan came back, the radio system was gone—an empty hole remained as the only memento of its existence. After this unfortunate event, the original door locks were replaced by reinforced versions which were harder to crack.

Break-ins like this happen every day, anywhere in the city and modified door locks were normal to me long ago. Why did they seem out of place now? The answer is that when you live in the U.S.A. long enough, you start getting *soft*. You start forgetting the "I should be careful at all times to be safe" mindset. Since everybody does it, you soon start leaving valuables in your car, walking on the streets without clinging to your purse, and overlooking the need to have metal bars protecting every window. This behavior is reinforced over time because it has no consequences, but in El Salvador if you are not always extra-careful you will pay for it. Even in the instances when you take precautions, something bad is bound to happen.

The second reminder of the security levels in this beautiful third world country came when we arrived at my friend's house. Even though Yolanda is not a rich movie star or an important politician, the entrance to her residential community was heavily guarded by not one, but three private security agents ready to shoot their firearms if needed. I later learned that a total of 16 private agents had been hired to protect and patrol the area 24 hours a day in order to ensure the well-being of the residents. It may sound excessive but, trust me, Salvadorians wouldn't be wasting their money on these things if they weren't absolutely necessary.

One of the entrances to my friend's residential community. Two armed guards can be seen in the picture. Visitors are required to provide a photo ID upon arrival which is then held by the sentries until the guests leave the premises.

With the reassurance that I couldn't be more protected in this quasi-military fortress, I spent the rest of the day celebrating with the future spouses and their friends. They were having a joint bachelor/bachelorette party and we all had a great time.

The Noise

The following morning I woke up to the voice of the city. It was a combination of loud buses' mufflers, doves, barking dogs, and reggaeton. After having lived in a small town surrounded by cornfields for over a year, I had forgotten what urban noise was really like. Despite having gone to bed past midnight I woke up spontaneously at 6 a.m. to the tune of blasting radios that welcomed me with candid lyrics: "*You drive me crazy when you grind against me baby, yeah yeah…*" With such great built-in surround sound, who needs an alarm clock?

The Cold Water Shower

After stretching and fully coming back to my senses I decided to abandon the coziness of my bed and get ready for the day. At the top of my list: taking a shower.

When I stay at Yolanda's I am fortunate because they have a boiler to heat water, which is not common in the country. El Salvador is warm enough to make water heating an unjustified expense. Growing up I had to take a cold shower every day. It is said that this practice increases longevity, but as a pre-teen I wasn't having it; I avoided showering like the plague and only caved in if my mother forced me.

As an adult I haven't had any problem with my ablutions, thanks in part to the long warm showers I've enjoyed since the day I moved to Mexico. Discovering the widespread use of hot water plumbing was life changing. I know my prolonged showers waste a lot of water and aren't ecological but I don't feel guilty about taking them. The way I see it, I'll most likely not have children, grandchildren, etc. and when we remove the environmental damage that all those people would do, I have enough green credit in my balance to afford a couple extra gallons per day—and then some.

I would have spent my typical 15 minutes of morning steamy happiness that day if it weren't for a small drawback. Unknown to me, Yolanda had decided to cut household expenses by turning off the boiler—it would be a cold shower for me this time ☹. I learned the news when I was ready and standing in the bathroom with my towel and respective toiletries. Good thing that…I'm an adult now…*sigh*

For all of you who'll ever be in this situation, either because your heating system breaks or you decide to go on a mission to an underdeveloped country, here are the tips on how to survive an icy cold shower:

Start by dipping your extremities, feet first preferably; then work your way up to the knees and continue with the hands, forearms, arms and thighs. Keep the shower stream low to avoid unnecessary pain in unprepared areas. After praying a little bit, you can proceed to bend forward and wet your head. By this time some drops will have inevitably sprinkled all over your body and acclimated you for what is to come.

I wish there were a special technique for wetting the torso but the best advice here is to "just do it." Increase the shower's flow a bit and quickly jump under the stream to finish as soon as possible. Emitting a loud scream will help you feel better, the same way it helps when you're riding down a very steep roller coaster. You will nearly pass out when the cold water hits you but, once the hyperventilation and shock subside, things will improve. Good luck!

The Food

Brrrr…with the shower out of the way, the next priority is breakfast. All those shivered-off calories need to be replaced!

A typical Salvadorian breakfast includes thick corn tortillas with refried beans, scrambled eggs, and "hard-soft" cheese (a local specialty). I wouldn't be too likely to find the brand of kefir and low-carb flax seed pita bread that I like to have in the mornings; food choices in general are not as vast and convenient as in the U.S.

This is not to say that Salvadorian food isn't good: I love the ceviches and homemade stews. I love anything that my aunts cook for me, like white bean soup, "Russian" salad, and *panes con chumpe* (a sort of turkey sandwich but three times better than what you're imagining). My mouth waters when I think about the desserts, the best desserts I've ever tasted! There are traditional local confections and European-style pastries full of meringue, fruit, cream, caramel and chocolate. We also have moist *tres leches* cakes and fig pies! Mmm…Salvadorian food *rocks*! I'm sure in heaven I'll have a never ending supply of all these treats!

Still, if I ever were to go back and live in El Salvador I'd have to keep in mind that my cooking style would have to change. Growing up, I don't remember having staples such as "steamable" vegetable bags and ready-to-eat frozen meals. I'd probably have to spend more time in the kitchen cooking from scratch. I would also have to haul propane gas tanks into the house as needed since there are not subterranean pipe lines to fuel the stoves.

Fortunately, for now, I'm just visiting.

A Kitchen Range
In The U.S.A.

Subterranean pipe lines offer continuous, uninterupted gas supplies.

A Kitchen Range
In El Salvador

Tanks have a limited amount of gas and must be replaced periodically with new ones.

The Political Campaigns

A full stomach makes for a happy heart. Once I've eaten my daily ration of tortillas I'm ready to go. My trip is short and there's a long list of people to visit before leaving!

I come out of Yolanda's guarded fortress and make my way through the streets of San Salvador. As I drive, I can't help but admire how beautiful the city naturally is (blessed weather, abundant flora) and how much better it could be without some of its little idiosyncrasies. For example, when I was little, there used to be a national "tradition" called *pinta y pega* (painting and gluing). Can you imagine what that is? It sounds like a kindergarten activity if you ask me, but the people involved were very much grownups. Here is what happened: every five years, large numbers of seemingly ordinary citizens would spontaneously gang up and form competing groups that raided the country in a perfectly orchestrated wave of destruction. The main objective of these groups was to outdo the others in marking every corner of the country with their respective logo. The team that glued and painted its emblem on the greatest amount of public surfaces was the winner. The gangs were very competitive and used every wall, bridge, gutter and public lighting post that crossed their way as a canvas to display their colors; even trees and stones were used as last resort. By the time they were done, the whole country had been upholstered.

The incredible thing about this tradition is that it was organized and carried out by the same governmental and political groups that eventually ended up leading the country. Every five years we had presidential elections, and this is the way the parties advertised.

Political campaigns in El Salvador always seemed crude, overwhelming, and disgusting to me. I remember pre-electoral months were a sequence of increasingly intruding radio, television, and newspaper ads with all the candidates attacking each other and lying about how great and honest they were. Between the media-bombarding and the pinta y pega, citizens had nowhere to hide. And since the political parties never cleaned up their messes, their graffiti and poster junk was left to pollute the cities indefinitely.

Even now, several years after the last electoral campaign, I can see numerous public places drowned under fading propaganda as I drive through San Salvador's streets.

Political Campaign Advertisement In The U.S.A.

- Little plastic signs are placed on front yards with the consent of the property owners.
- Signs are temporary and can be easily removed once the electoral campaign is over.

Political Campaign Advertisement In El Salvador

- When I lived in the country, the most evident trait of a political campaign was known as "pinta y pega" (painting and gluing). The practice involved the use of public (and sometimes private) spaces by political parties who'd go wild painting and gluing their logos throughout the country.
- Nobody cleaned up after the end of the campaigns.

⇩ Political Graffiti

The Crazy Traffic

Did I say I was driving through San Salvador? I meant to say I was stuck in traffic!

The capital's roadway system is a wild jungle, and like any other jungle, it is ruled by the principle of survival of the fittest. I don't know if it's related to the population's general frustrations over a failing economy or if it's just a lack of law enforcement, but everybody drives as if competing in a life-or-death satanic race.

Back in the day I used to be a fierce contestant, you didn't want to mess with teen-Alex! During traffic jams, I knew how to drive no more than one foot away from the car in front of me to prevent "the enemy" from stealing my place in line. It required a great deal of concentration, since every acceleration and brake had to be perfectly timed to avoid a collision, but it worked wonders to deter the vulture taxi drivers who were always trying to cut in. I also had a gift for weaving in and out of lanes between cars, and I did it with such professional grace that even Speedy Gonzales would have been jealous.

That was then. Now I'm 30 and softened up by the incredibly respectful U.S. way of driving. I can't handle savage traffic anymore and, if given the choice, I ask friends to drive instead of me. When I see drivers launching their vehicles towards pedestrians, I'm horrified; and I can't get used to the outbursts of group-rage and *La Vieja* honks behind me every time I stop to yield at crosswalks (even pedestrians look suspiciously at me when I stop to let them pass).

The fascination that city drivers have with their horns is beyond me. It may be some sort of phallic symbol or a way to feel powerful, who knows; but there's an abundance of neurotic drivers out there who think cars are driven by honking instead of by steering the wheel. What's more, the horn is believed to have magical qualities that allow its users to control other cars as well; and so, as soon as the traffic light turns green, everybody starts honking to get the first vehicle in line moving.

Unfortunately, the horns don't have an immediate effect, because the leader of the line is *deliberately* waiting a few seconds before moving forward. Why? Because in El Salvador when the traffic light changes to orange, drivers don't think "The light is about to turn red, I should start decreasing my speed" no, what they think is "*Hijue*! The light is about to turn red! I better accelerate this

Let's Learn Some Lingo

"La Vieja" honk = a special way of horn honking which attest to the cleverness of Salvadorian drivers who needed a way to insult others without getting out of their cars. They found out that by honking their horns three times following a particular rhythm (*Beep-beep Beeeep*), they could convey the message "La Vieja de tu p**a madre!" (which means "Your old f***ing mother!") without saying a word. How is that for resourcefulness?

"Hijue!" = short for "Hijo de tu _ madre" or "son of your _ mother." Used as a mild expression of surprise, worry, etc.

piece of junk or I won't make it!" Consequently, by the time the light turns red, there's a high chance that a couple of vehicles will still be crossing (or about to cross) the intersection. Therefore, a wise Salvadorian driver knows that green is not an indication to move forward, it is an indication to make sure the intersection is clear and only when that is confirmed can he proceed.

All the honking, the racing, the sense of urgency seems to be based on an inner need to move faster than everybody else—to show who's the boss! And in a land where the stronger prevails, bigger vehicles make for bolder drivers. First we have motorcyclists whose vehicles are too small to scare anyone. Since they cannot attack, their niche is to sneak in the middle of jammed cars and move ahead of the crowd while everyone envies their lane-splitting abilities. Next in the food chain come small sedans, both privately owned and taxis, which have an advantage because their drivers don't always own the units and thus don't care too much about scratches or small bumps. They will appear out of nowhere and try to cut in almost perpendicularly between you and the car ahead, you will have to let them get away with it unless you're willing to risk a collision with a (most likely uninsured) driver who will never pay for your damages (OR, you can learn to drive bumper-to-bumper with the car in front of you!). Sedans and pickup trucks are ranked fairly close together, but the latter have the ability to handle rougher terrain. When bottlenecks get too unbearable, pickup trucks readily get out of paved lanes and use the shoulders to get to the front of the line where they force their way back in. Eventually, a whole new lane is formed on the shoulder and the congestion is therefore intensified.

Moving upward along the food chain we find micro-buses. These are wicked hybrids resulting from the mating of taxis with pickup trucks. They have inherited the shoulder-driving and perpendicular-attack abilities of their parents but their greater size (due to a genetic mutation) makes them more dangerous.

Finally, at the very top of the chain we have public buses...and here dear reader, you need to beware, be *very* aware! Full-sized buses are indisputable kings of the road; don't *ever* dream of challenging their power or you *will* be sorry. Public buses in El Salvador are free to do whatever they please: stop in the middle of the street to load passengers, drive toward your car as if you weren't there, ram you out of your lane, ANYTHING. And for your own good, please! LET THEM!!!! That's the law of the jungle!

Vehicular Specimens

King of the Jungle ⇧

A Road Shoulder In The U.S.A.

- Road shoulders remain clear of vehicular traffic so as to be available in case of emergency.

A Road Shoulder In El Salvador

- Shoulders are commonly [ab]used by drivers as an additional lane during traffic congestions.
- The government had to build a series of short posts on this street's shoulder in order to keep it clear of traffic (rendering the shoulder unusable during emergencies).
- Do you remember El Espino (pg. 10)? This used to be part of it.

Transit Authority
In The U.S.A.

Specially trained personnel help maintain the fluidity of traffic when needed.

Transit Authority
In El Salvador

When policemen are not available, resourceful Salvadorians see an opportunity to earn extra income. Dressed as clowns or superheroes (or superhero-clowns as pictured here) they post themselves at crowded intersections to direct the traffic in exchange for occasional tips from drivers.

The Joie De Vivre*

By now I probably have scared you pretty badly. I don't think you're feeling too excited about spending your next vacation in San Salvador—and I don't blame you. I have used this book to highlight some of the most striking differences between El Salvador and the U.S. and, sadly, those differences aren't too favorable for the former.

Although I can't deny that safety, order, and infrastructure in my hometown are poor…and living in the country doesn't seem too desirable either (as the exodus we're experiencing attests), I must stress that from a purely *touristic* point of view El Salvador is a paradise. It has *extremely* friendly, kind, and helpful people; SUPERB food; breathtaking landscapes…the list goes on and on. One of my aunts reminded me about this fact when I visited her last time; instead of our customary evening of tea and cookies, Aunt Clarita wanted to go to the beach.

Clarita is one of my two adoptive aunts. She and Aunt Sarita were my Mom's best friends and I grew up visiting them regularly. I love them both to pieces! Even when we don't share a common lineage, the coziness of their affection has taught me that blood ties don't necessarily mean a thing. As a matter of fact, since Mom died I've received the deepest wounds from family members while the most unconditional support has come from non-relatives.

Aunt Clarita is a very wise lady whose age you would never guess. If such a thing as the fountain of youth exists, she has surely drank from it. When people ask her what is her secret for her everlasting glow she answers that "it's all about being happy and taking things one day at a time."

Aunt Clarita does everything according to the principle of the "quality of life." What this means is that she enjoys the good things she has while she has them and while they are at their prime. When Mom was saving the silver-plated knives, forks and spoons for "special" occasions, my aunt convinced her to use them every day. Not only did my mother listen, but we ended up having meals on the "good" china and drinking water from crystal cups. Had Mom not done this, she'd have died without ever using her stuff.

When Aunt Clarita found the city traffic too unbearable and the price of gas too high, what did she do? She *sold* her car and used the money to travel through Europe. Now she carpools with a friend to her part-time job and, when she wants to go out, she hires a taxi driver. Since she's a frequent customer who gets a special rate, she's able to afford a private chauffer with no car maintenance worries and no driving stress—isn't she smart?

The day she took me to the beach, I remembered that this life is more than deadlines; we all need to stop and smell the roses sometime. Aunt Clarita and I went to an exclusive club where we got our own waitress and a private cabin meters away from the sea. Yes, it was expensive, but it was also an once-in-a-lifetime experience and we split the bill.

As I sunbathed on my hammock enjoying a shrimp cocktail, I couldn't avoid wondering: why can't life always be this way?

*The Joy of Life

A Beach
In The U.S.A.

- White sand.
- Weather / water can get freezing cold during winter.

A Beach
In El Salvador

- Black sand, most likely due to the volcanic nature of the region.
- Weather / water is always deliciously warm.

The Flirts

After a splendid day at the beach, Aunt Clarita and I were ready to return to the city. Right before sunset, we packed our belongings and made our way back home. As we drove away from the shore all I wanted to do was to open the window and immerse myself in the moment. I wanted to smell the tangy scent of the sea, let the breeze play with my hair, and share in the peacefulness of the cows that grazed so freely along the road. For some strange reason, everything at that moment felt special, magical! It may have been iodine poisoning from the two pounds of shrimp I had just eaten; or a vitamin D overdose after years of gloomy-cubicle dwelling but whatever the reason, being alive felt great!

The only thing keeping our taxi's window from falling apart was a piece of wood.

I was about to open my window when I noticed a wooden wedge propped against the glass. I asked our chauffer about the nature of the wedge and he explained that the cranking mechanism of the window had been broken some time ago when thieves tried to force it open. The wedge was the only thing keeping the glass from falling and, needless to say, opening the window was out of the question. Destiny had decided that there would be no magical "wind-in-the-hair" moment for me...I would have to settle for looking through the windshield instead.

And that's when I saw it...

Moving in front of us there was this strange mass of people mysteriously floating above the floor. *What the heck was that???*

I had to look again to fully understand the nature of the apparition. During all my years living in El Salvador I had *never* seen something like this.

Upon closer examination, what had seemed to be a mere illusion turned out to be a ramshackle pickup truck loaded to the brim—and beyond—with people. Un-be-lie-va-ble. The passengers looked like anchovy fillets tightly canned in salty oil. At least 20 traveled on the bed of the vehicle while six risked their lives riding *on the bumper.* I'm not exaggerating. The vehicle overflowed and barely moved due to the excessive weight. I was in disbelief.

Our taxi driver found my astonishment comical and went on to explain that overcrowded vehicles like that were a normal way of public transportation in the area. I don't know how I'd missed them before (I must have been very busy talking with my aunt) but now that I looked out the windows it was true, the trucks where everywhere! What a scene…I HAD to take a picture!

Like a heroine in an action movie I asked the driver to "follow that truck!" Then I grabbed my camera and shot it like a paparazzo who's just found Kim Kardashian wearing a thong. The images taken through the windshield were blurry and I wanted better so, as soon as the truck made a stop, I asked our driver to pull off the road and I ran out of the cab like a crazy lady. All I wanted was to capture the unbelievable image in all its splendor and nothing else mattered. I continued to walk closer and closer to my target, taking pictures with every step but, in doing so, I completely forgot that I wasn't wearing my invisibility cloak! The people riding the truck (mostly men) were very able to see me and, as soon as I was close enough, they hurled me with piropos.

A human ball "floated" in front of our car. It turned out to be a pickup truck overloaded with people—normal way of transportation in the area. My eagerness to capture the image in film inadvertedly got me closer to the group. When the guys saw me, they started flirting and blowing kisses at me.

"Piropos" are words. To be more specific, piropos are the words that a male brain chooses to utter when it wants to express a penis' thoughts. Interestingly enough, I cannot come up with a single English term to fully convey the meaning of piropo. You could say it translates as "compliment" or "flirtatious remark" but you'd be missing the intrinsic naughty-friskiness of the whole situation.

A typical Salvadorian piropo takes place when a woman with no missing body parts walks outdoors in the vicinity of a group of men. When she's close enough, a primal reproductive instinct kicks in and the guys' endocrine systems go into overdrive. A rush of adrenaline is released into the bloodstream and pumped into the brain where it messes up with the normal use of the hippocampus. Everything goes downhill from there. With their brain impaired, men forget the existence of good manners, the virtues of restraint, proper language, and all sorts of baloney starts coming out of their mouths.

Whistles, "sssh, ssh, sshh" sounds, and humorous romantic phrases are the standard during a piropos session. It is important to stress that the things going through the minds of "piropeadores" when they produce these noises are not innocent; in fact, the thoughts can be so dirty that even impaired brains realize they should not be said out loud. Since it would be too embarrassing to say things as they are, piropeadores have mastered the creative use of metaphors. For example, a gentleman may have a clear

*kiss*kiss*
Mamacita rica!
⇩

image of where he would like his tongue to be, but instead of stating it clearly, he says: "*Mamasota*! [big momma] How *rica* [yummy] you are! Mmmm…I would like to eat from your pupusa[34] *miamorrrr* [my love] and later have a taste of those *coquitos* [little coconuts] of yours *mamacita* [lil' mama]." Sometimes the words used are so colloquially obscure that the only way the message can be understood is if the piropeador and the person receiving the piropo have a common linguistic background.

There is an ongoing debate on whether the use of piropos constitutes a charming folkloric practice or a badly disguised chauvinist behavior. Feminist groups maintain that the openly sexual comments denigrate women, objectify them, and continue to promote the female status as submissive to men. Particularly alarming is the fact that men don't show good judgment when it comes to "piroping" young women and are often found targeting barely pubescent girls. The things the guys say to these girls can often include phrases which would clearly be grounds for sexual harassment charges in developed countries.

In my opinion the practice is as primitive and out of place in this day and age as believing that women enjoy doing housework just because they are women or that a woman who goes out on the street wearing a mini skirt "is asking to be raped" (heard many times in El Salvador, Mexico, and the U.S.). Comments like these only attest to an abysmal degree of ignorance and cultural underdevelopment of the speaker and should be treated as the stupidities they are. Luckily, women are not powerless to address the situation and, as a matter of fact, they have the most effective tool to educate their men. Simply put, the world we now know is one where a man will *always* be born from a woman, and as mothers, women are in the ideal position to inculcate true values and respect.

At the end of the day I only wonder, when guys start howling on the street like a pack of wolves…what is their purpose? Do they really think someone is going to fall for it? Honestly, who's going to end up dating the lascivious guy that salivates uncontrollably as he screams how delicious your ____ is and all the dirty things he would like to do with it? Also, what is their fixation with their "mamis"? Mami you are this, mami I would like to eat your that, mamasota here and there. It is a mystery to me. In the meantime, every time I hear them, I keep walking.

It's So Good To Be Here!

Time certainly flies when you're having fun, and just when I was getting used to living in a never ending tropical vacation, the dates on my planner indicated that it was time to go back to the U.S.

Leaving the country that saw you grow is always bittersweet…for immigrants in search of a decent future, it is mostly bitter. It's sad to leave a place where you naturally "fit in," a place where the first thing that people see when they meet you is not your race and where you're not automatically perceived as a second class citizen. At the same time, it is comforting to know that you're migrating to a healthier environment; that you'll live in a slightly more civilized society where laws are taken seriously and car locks don't have to be reinforced to prevent robberies… Then again, it is sad to realize your homeland is in such bad shape that you're forced to leave it and all your loved ones with it… It's complicated…

---

34 The meaning of pupusa was explained on page 29.

When I came back to the U.S., my first thought was "no more mosquitoes" (yeah!). Upon arriving I was able to sleep all night and, surprisingly, woke up at 11 a.m. instead of 6 a.m. Not having all the noise really made a difference.

For several days I thought about the internal conflict of immigrants' desires, the dichotomy between staying and leaving one's homeland. I don't know what goes on in other people's heads but, personally, the more time passes the more I realize my childhood memories are all but gone, nothing is left of them in El Salvador. The places I once knew have changed and so have the people, I don't even know where the holes on the street are anymore...I guess it was inevitable: the longing to go back to my roots is fading and I feel more and more like a U.S. citizen every day.

I will never stop loving El Salvador. Despite all the crime and its generalized chaos, the land will always have a special place in my heart. Growing up there I learned about humility and self-respect, street-smarts and critical thinking. I also learned that the most valuable possessions a person can have are not available for sale...I don't know why but—for the first time since I started writing this book—these words make me want to cry. Actually, I don't want to, I just do. But I wipe the solitary tear that is about to escape through the corner of my eye and I keep on typing.

It seems that I will end up being one more who intended to come to the U.S. "for a couple years only" but then never left. The U.S.A. is indeed a great country. And as I unpacked my belongings after returning from my trip, I told the friend who was accompanying me: "You know what? The more I go to my home country nowadays, the sooner I want to come back to the States."

The American Dream   Chapter 9

"You'll have dreams and you'll go to someone and you'll say, 'This is a great idea.' And that person will say, 'No, it isn't. And you have to go back to your cubicle. Now the question is, who do you believe?" —Bill Cosby

The American Dream can mean something different for each one of us. To me, it is the idea that in America there's always something better for those who are willing to work for it. It is the hope that finding our personal happiness here is possible; the belief that in the U.S.A. we are free to pursue that which we are passionate about— knowing that we actually have a chance to succeed at it.

As I write these words, I have been a "freelancer" for almost a year. From the day I came back from my trip to El Salvador, I have been working day and night to create this manuscript and, let me tell you, I've enjoyed every second of it! Besides writing, I've started developing a patent idea for a product that could potentially reduce paper waste. If the idea works, it would allow me to make a tiny contribution to our economy while helping our environment.

I don't know how any of my projects are going to end, but I know their outcomes will not be limited by lack of effort. I am aware that my current "self-employment" status can only last for as long as my savings, and I am running out of time; however, I am convinced that our existence can only make sense if we love what we do, and I want a shot at it! I don't want to look back in time when I'm older and wonder "what if" I had followed my heart.

Although there have been many difficult times in my journey, I am thankful for everything that's happened, because each one of those experiences has shaped me into the person I am now. Going through so much has also helped me understand this world better. I have come to the conclusion that the system this world is based on functions in a way in which we, regular people, end up being an instrument for the prosperity of those at the top. From the moment we're sent to school, we unknowingly enter an invisible assembly line that produces workers. We go through different molding stations (primary school, high school) where we're psychologically shaped to become ideal laborers for the benefit of the supreme whole. This system has been effective in maintaining order. Some could argue it is necessary for our society to function, and that could very well be the case (I don't know); however, the problem is that we're losing our humanity in the process. What the individual wants is not a priority anymore, only the needs of the collective.

We need to wake up, **WAKE UP!!!** And realize that there is absolutely *no one* out there caring about *our* happiness: if we want it we have to chase it ourselves.

I know I may be crazy for leaving my corporate job and choosing to follow such an uncertain road. I'm also aware my goals are ambitious but, if we want to reach the American Dream, shouldn't we start by dreaming?

Am I Greedy For Wanting More?

In this time of global economic crisis when roughly half of recent college graduates in the U.S. are having trouble finding proper jobs,[35] I know some people may criticize my decision to abandon corporate America. Some may even call me ungrateful for not appreciating such great opportunity and I respect their opinions. But if it didn't make me happy, what was the purpose of staying? Just to be safe? Avoid ever being afraid? Is that what we should really strive for?

Yes, I feel guilty when I admit I wasn't satisfied with the prospects I had. I feel especially bad when I think of all the illegal immigrants who risk their lives to come here just to end up spending their whole existence hiding in the shadows. They would die to have half of what I gave away. Still, I don't think that should stop me from dreaming of having what I really want.

And the question remains: Am I greedy for wanting more? Should I conform to having less than what I want just because what I already have is so much more than what millions of Hispanics can only dream of? Am I selfish? Am I repulsively ambitious?

Let me ask you something else: Would it be OK for me to want more if I was a "young American man"? Would I still be ungrateful then? Or would the word "ambitious" take on a different, positive meaning like "spirited," "goal oriented," or "visionary" instead of "greedy"?

A wealthy U.S. gentleman once told me: "*If Hispanic immigrants don't like their life here, they can go home; nobody asked them to come.*" Yes, he's right, nobody asked me to come. But what if the U.S. is my home? Where should I go? Should I not be allowed to dream big here just because I'm Hispanic? I refuse to accept his reasoning. I choose to believe that I can aspire to reach happiness here (or anywhere) just because I am a person, period—no racial strings attached. And if I ever dislike my life here, I don't think leaving is the only answer; I can also work to improve my situation, fight for my personal goals, and not settle for less.

An "American Thing"

You could think I'm arrogant and I would understand it. After all, who do I think I am to deserve more? Well, let me see…for starters, I think I am a human being lucky enough to live in a country full of opportunities. I don't think there's something particularly special about me; I'm just one more, like you and everybody else. But it's precisely in that commonness where the deeper truth resides. I firmly believe that each and every one of us is *entitled* to want more and go for it, regardless of race, age, gender, or socioeconomic level—and we should not be apologizing for it. "More" doesn't necessarily mean material possessions or increased credit card debt to buy more stuff, no! It can simply mean finding a fulfilling life you feel is worth living, an occupation where you use your abilities in tasks of real value to you. In other words, "more" can mean finding a balance between working for the benefit of the system, the benefit of others, and for the benefit of YOU.

---

35 Courtney Subramanian, 2012. Half of New College Grads Jobless or Underemployed. *Time Newsfeeds*. Available from: http://newsfeed.time.com/2012/04/23/half-of-new-college-grads-jobless-or-underemployed/. Accessed on: 4/17/2013

Wanting to better our existence is a fundamental part of living in the U.S.A., a basic step in declaring our independence: independence from mistaken preconceptions others may have about us, freedom from errors we may have committed in the past, and total liberty to choose where we aim our future.

I know I'm not an authority to be telling you anything so, in case you don't believe me, allow me to cite our *Declaration of Independence*. It was written by a group of outstanding gentlemen who undoubtedly knew what they were talking about. It says:

> *"We hold these truths to be self-evident, that all men are created equal, that they are endowed by their Creator with certain unalienable Rights, that among these are Life, Liberty and **the pursuit of Happiness**."*

"The pursuit of happiness," you see? The most important document in The United States of America recognizes the importance of the want, the need, the *right* to pursue our happiness. And if what you have right now is not making you happy, wouldn't it be the most "American" thing to want more?

Chapter 10   To ALL Of America With Love

Dear American People:

The first chapter in this book is solely dedicated to the citizens of The United States of America who so kindly allowed me into their land. The message of this last chapter though, is a little broader.

For some reason which I still don't comprehend, upon my arrival to the U.S.A. people would often ask me: "So, when did you first come to America?"…and I didn't know what to say. They probably thought I was a little slow when I couldn't answer such a simple question, but I honestly didn't understand. The reason of my confusion was this: I was born in *Central America*. The way I see it, I've been American all my life!

It turns out that people often reserve the term "America" for referring to the U.S.A. alone. In the country where I come from, the word "America" is used to denote the mass of land extending south of the Arctic Ocean all the way down to the Patagonia, and encompassing everything in between. Please don't hate me for bringing this up but, even for the greatest nation I've ever seen, isn't it a tiny little bit disdainful to consider that "America" means one single country?

Now, with that clarification out of the way, you'll understand when I say that this last chapter is dedicated to *all* of America, United States and beyond.

***

When I first started writing, I intended this to be a happy book; one to laugh about the huge differences between my two beloved countries: the one I come from and the one I now belong to. In all honesty, to me it was funny to see clowns directing traffic in El Salvador, packs of dogs making their home in our National University, and people stealing manhole covers off the street but…as I finish this book, I feel a profound sadness. I realize that the life many of my Salvadorian brothers and sisters have is not worthy of them, is not worthy of any human. It angers me to finally understand this: that in order for our current social structure to exist, poor people *must* exist also. And the system *will* make sure (either consciously or not) that this continues to be the case. Think about it, if we were all millionaires, who would clean someone else's house? Who would pick up someone else's trash? It angers and saddens me because I feel so powerless and there's nothing I can do about this. I don't even know if global equality is even possible; we humans have a tendency to move away from it, just look at our history.

Since global equality may be a little too out of my hands, I'll be happy if I'm just able to transmit a few messages. **To U.S. citizens: <u>don't forget how lucky you are.</u>** Don't forget how good you have it. Feel blessed for all the things bestowed on you and for all that you're *free of*, all the worries you'll never have simply because you were born or allowed on this side of the border. I don't say this in an accusatory tone, not at all, this is actually very positive. I just want you to realize your luck so that you can be a little happier with what you already have because, believe me, it's plenty. I promise you, that 50" LED television that is making you miserable because you can't have it, would be totally irrelevant if you lived in a shack with no electricity—and if you save well enough, you will soon have it. Also please **<u>remember that The United States of America is a land that has thrived on immigration.</u>** It was founded by settlers who came from the "old world," grew strong with the hard work of numerous cultures, and continues to be a top player internationally thanks in part to its vast cultural diversity which is key in an era of globalization. Believing that Hispanic immigrants in the U.S.A. are here only to "soak up public funds like sponges with no desire to give back," or that they are "criminals responsible for all of the U.S. drug and delinquency problems" denotes a lack of understanding of the big picture and is a hasty judgment based on partial information. I've met many immigrants while in this country, and all of them worked harder than you'd imagine.

To the immigrants, legal or not, my advice to you would be to **<u>respect this country</u>**. Even if you grew up (as I did) in the middle of a corrupt society, where bending the rules to get the most out of every situation seems like a normal practice, please don't. It is not normal. Our home countries' situations are not normal. We can do better. Try to respect the laws in this country because it is precisely the order instilled by them that allows our life here to be so great. Never forget to be grateful for all the freedom, the safety and the chances you're given in this admirable land and try to behave in a way that will allow future generations to enjoy the same opportunities. **<u>Never forget *why* you decided to come</u>** nor all that you left behind to be here. Please don't waste your time or your life. You may feel lonely but if you fall into alcohol or drugs to compensate, the money you were going to save to build your house and help your family back in your country, all or most of it is going to be lost. Remember that at this exact moment in time at least one person is thinking about crossing the border; and many will lose their life in that pursuit.

Let's face it. Hispanic immigrants are not always welcomed in the United States, especially the ones that come illegally. A quick browsing session on the internet is enough to witness the unabashed hatred that the topic of immigration is capable of inciting. Being who I am and having lived through what I have, I understand perfectly well both sides of the coin. And let me tell you: both sides are right.

Hispanic people are right in trying to better their life and their children's. As long as conditions in our third world countries continue to be as horrid as they are and as long as immigrants continue to find work, a decent life, and amnesty in the U.S., it makes all the sense for them to come. Yes, it is true that some break the law when they cross the border; but I bet that if you or I, or anybody else was in their shoes, we would also consider the option.

On the other hand, U.S. citizens are *also* right. Somebody crossing their borders illegally is no different from someone who breaks into your house at night without being invited. They have all the right to defend and protect their borders and have no obligation to modify their country's laws or customs to accommodate the needs of illegal residents. The word "illegal" when used to denominate people sounds ugly, sounds criminal, and may be objectionable, but it is merely the truth. Like in any other country, the internal laws and policies put forward in the U.S. should be made so that they are, above all, beneficial for the country itself, while remembering that "with great power comes great responsibility."

I know that what I'm saying may be considered controversial and I don't want to lose any friends by expressing my views...but I don't want to remain silent either.

I once showed this book to a prominent U.S. businessman. Despite his busy agenda, the gentleman had the kindness to browse through the material and share his honest opinion with me. He started by saying how easy we immigrants want to have it (I doubt he's ever worked shoulder to shoulder with immigrants in say, a greenhouse, or cleaning a doughnut factory) and how ungrateful we are for not being satisfied with what we have (I suspect he wouldn't be too conformist either, judging from his entrepreneurial spirit). After he talked for a few minutes, he finished by saying: "When it comes to migration, you guys should learn to emulate the behaviors of my forefathers, those whose efforts made America the great nation it is today." I believe he meant the part where the forefathers worked hard to make this country the land of wonders it is today; one that strives for equality, liberty, and opportunity for all...but I could not avoid thinking that, if modern immigrants were really to emulate the *migration* approach followed by the very first American settlers, they would have to come armed with superior weaponry to eradicate most of the current inhabitants, enslave or exploit the survivors, and declare themselves the righteous owners of the land—not a desirable picture. After that chat I decided not to show this book anymore until it was finished, and now the time has come...

There was a day when I learned that there were people living on landfills in my hometown, children who fed from the trash. I was a teen back then, but I was very surprised to realize that if nobody had told me, I would have never found out. Something so relevant was happening right next to me and I was oblivious. After that day I realized that it is SO important for us to know the full extent of the reality we live in, including the way this reality looks like for others: if we—as a nation—ignore our own shortcomings, there is nothing we can do to effectively change.

Because the first step is understanding, I give this book to you.

Love,

America

In The U.S.A.

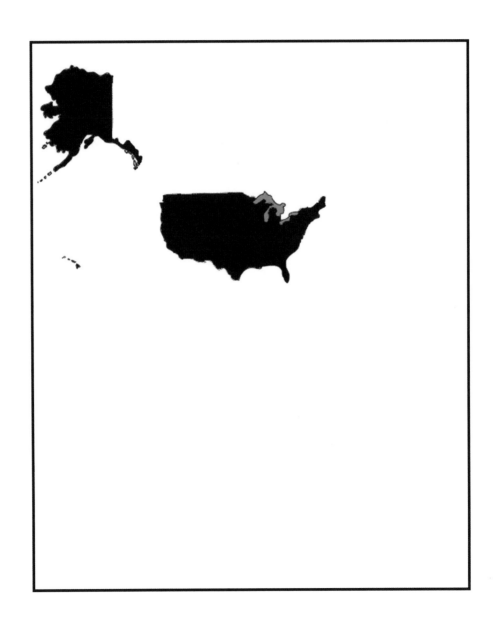

America

In El Salvador

El Salvador

Peace.

About The Author

With Chinese, Panamanian, and Salvadorian heritage, Alejandra Campos is a Hispanic voice like no other.

Her polemic views on the subject of migration are a direct result of her personal experiences while living in El Salvador (one of the most violent countries in America), Mexico, and the United States of America.

Traveling the world from a very young age, Alejandra settled in the United States and eventually became a naturalized citizen. Although her legal status has always been legitimate, her "adventures" in this country have mirrored that of illegal aliens in many ways.

Alejandra's outstanding academic background includes an Industrial Engineering degree, a M.S. in Food Science and multiple academic awards.